First Edition

PREFERRING SOCIALISM OVER DEMOCRACY

Envisioning Cities of Societal Harmony & Continual Coexistence

JAN FREDERICK SK
(AUTHOR)

Table Of Contents

Can Be Found Starting On
The Right Side Or Next Page

TABLE OF CONTENTS

SECTION C

SECTION D

SECTION E

Opening Quote

Preferring Socialism Over Democracy :
Envisioning Cities Of Societal Harmony &
Continual Coexistence

"I hope that this book will be sent to all corners of the world for the sake of a conquest of the world, that yearns to change the mindset of the world to realizing what this book ultimately provides — information that will turn the hearts of the children to their fathers and also vice versa, that will bring about a form of coexistence as likewise has been the core foundations of the universe and all the elements therein. I carry a bow with the means to shoot arrows filled with values and understandings to the minds of the world. Allow me to do this conquest of goodness to achieve and bring the world to the understanding of goodness itself."

Preface

Preferring Socialism Over Democracy :
Envisioning Cities Of Societal Harmony &
Continual Coexistence

I BELIEVE THAT many people dislike socialism and that the world was made to appreciate democracy. This book is a pro-socialist book and the only way I could get people who hate socialism to change their mindset is to tell them the following.

Every good leader with a good healthy mind would want his people / citizens not to suffer while they live out their lives as citizens of the country but the fact is that in any form of government, citizens may end up suffering — there is that usual possibility. We know this because people suffer in both non-authoritative countries and authoritative countries for various reasons, some are caused by governments, others are caused by their fellow citizens.

The way I see it, no matter how good / good-hearted a leader is, if he rules using democracy, there is a limit to the goodness that he can provide for his citizens. There is no possible way for him to defend every good citizen from the hearts of wicked men. But by use of an authoritative system / ideology, a good-hearted leader can protect every single righteous living individual from wickedness coming from the people around them.

Both the bad & the good of using authoritative systems is that the system follows the characteristics and being of the leader. If the leader is wickedness incarnate, the people will automatically suffer. But if the leader is righteous and holy, just and loving, the good people in the country will prosper while the wicked will be living in discomfort.

I am sure that you are aware that I use the words, 'wickedness' and 'righteous' to describe people. I believe that every person is born caring and loving. The only reason a baby becomes a devil is because something happened in his life that changes his attitude towards others. Every person is born with a heart and every heart can turn wicked — there is always that possibility. Every person is born with a percentage of craziness / mental disorder — that percentage is never zero. The only difference between a psychopath and a regular person is that the percentage of craziness of the psychopath is more than that of a regular person. Theoretically, there is always something wrong with any given person, no one is mentally stable.

This is who I am. A Christian & a Socialist; a dreamer & a writer. Whoever believes what I believe in the previous paragraph should at least be a forgiving person or a person who is willing to forgive.

The goal of this book is to give awareness to the fact that Socialism isn't as bad as how the world was made to believe. Like I said, an authoritative system isn't a bad system. The ruler of the country governs the country based on his values meaning that if it ends up a bad system, it would be the leader's fault. Whereas in a democratic system, the leader could be a good person but he has limits. A bad ruling system is a system that limits the actions of the ruler.

It might sound strange to the reader that a system consisting of freedom (democracy), is not as good as an authoritative one. We will discuss this as we move forward. But having a form of restriction is better than allowing freedom. If every single one of us is righteous and holy, we may not need to care about which system is best. But because amongst humanity, there exists those who **chooses** to walk the path of wickedness / people who live by inappropriate values, therefore, restrictions are the best way to go.

FIRST GRAND CHAPTER : THE KNOWLEDGE & UNDERSTANDINGS OF SOCIALISM

Preferring Socialism Over Democracy : Envisioning Cities Of Societal Harmony & Continual Coexistence

I. Common Misunderstandings About Socialism

FIRST GRAND CHAPTER : THE KNOWLEDGE & UNDERSTANDINGS OF SOCIALISM

WHEN PEOPLE HEAR the word Socialism, these things come to mind : anti-freedom, authoritative, forceful, thieves, liars, dictatorships, restrictive, non-democratic, utopian societies, harmful, making slaves out of people, filled with simple and naive thinkers, causing hypcrinflation, and all the other things that happen when you place a simple & naive thinker as a leader of a country. Socialism may be some if not all of these things to most people, but when seen from a different angle, people may find that there are reasons as to why these misunderstandings appear.

Most people dislike socialism because they have firsthand experience with leaders of socialism and its many forms. But what I want the reader to briefly understand is that there is a difference between the leader and the ideology that he or she uses. An ideology is a set of ideas and ideals that makes up a system and this system is fixed. Systems are mostly created to better the lives of people, created from the understandings of the one who made them. Whereas a human being is not static in nature. Human beings are dynamic in a sense that they can change with time. A good guy, in the beginning, may become a villain at the end. A humble man through the gifts of riches and power may turn into a man filled with pride and arrogance. Some of us have elected what we believe to be good people but later in their lives are indicted with corruption charges. We do see famous child actors that turned into drug addicts because of the people they surround themselves with. What all these examples are trying to tell you is that people change. They act on their emotions or impulses. Leaders are people and they have egos; sometimes they do not conform to the ideologies that they use. They have wives and advisors that change their way of thought. These things affect everyone. But it does not mean that when a socialist leader does something despicable, therefore Socialism is the root cause of that despicable act.

Another similar issue that may be much easier to understand concerning the difference between the leader and the ideology that is used, is the difference between a person and his or her religion. When a person does a bad thing and people know his or her religion, I have found some people to blame the religion. But is this a fact? Does a man who rapes mean that whichever religion he studies, advocates rape? I hope we all agree that the answer is no. Likewise, should it be seen when we talk about the difference between the leader and the ideology that is being used.

Another eye-opening fact is that there is a difference between (1) a Socialist who calls himself one because he likes reading about Socialism and finds it more attractive than all the other ideologies and (2) a person whose way of thinking conforms to Socialism without having to study about it, in other words, the character of the person is Socialism itself or at least to the most of it. **This will be discussed in later chapters**.

In the first paragraph, we talked about the misunderstandings as viewed by people who have personal encounters with Socialism. In this paragraph, we come to see the misunderstandings of people with a little bit of intellect, those who like reading and talking about economic and political issues. To them, Socialism, Communism, and Marxism are all talking about the same things, the only difference being, their names.

I have to agree that all three ideologies, Socialism, Communism, and Marxism, do have similar goals but they have differences. One of their differences is how they achieve the goal they planned on achieving. A simple example is this. How does a man learn something he has yet to understand? (1) He gets himself a teacher, (2) he learns it himself by going to the library, or (3) he tries to understand it without using techniques 1 and 2, also known as self-teaching. My question is, which is the longest process, which is the fastest process? The fastest is hiring a teacher. The longest process is self-teaching. The next question is what is the difference between learning by getting the information from someone else, and learning by trying to do it yourself. Which one gives you an understanding and which one gives you a form of wisdom?

Let me give you my definition of wisdom. Wisdom is hard-earned knowledge. It is in most cases obtained through thorough experience of doing something again and again all the while obtaining lessons along the way. And those lessons may help us to prevent silly mistakes in the future. One drawback about wisdom is that it is difficult to pass on the experience to your children. One can pass on information derived through wisdom but it will not stop your children from going against the teaching you have given them, out of their own curiosity.

Coming back to answering the question. Having obtained factual results when earned through self-teaching leads to wisdom while receiving information from someone else begets knowledge. In this case, the process by which the result is achieved matters as it may in most cases have an impact on the result. Now, I am pointing out that the process by which Socialism, Communism, or Marxism is achieved respectively are different, in that very same way.

Because of all these misunderstandings about Socialism, many people end up following the crowd in rendering Socialism as something evil, or as something that should be avoided. If I may tell the reader a bit about myself, I am a Christian, I am a Socialist, and I very much care about the well-being of the people. But the moment I utter the word Socialism, no matter the context, I am shunned by some groups of people, even amongst the Christian community.

Some countries have past unpleasant experiences with Socialism or its other forms and when political parties form under such a name, problems tend to arise for that particular party. Because the media will also attack Socialism when such a thing shows up in the country, the people are affected in such a way that they also end up viewing socialism with the same spectacles as how the media portrays Socialism to be. I live in a country that is of this kind. That being said, three groups of people are against Socialism, (1) government bodies, (2) secular people, & (3) religious groups. And all these people dislike socialism because of their misunderstandings of it.

Currently, the reader should have a brief understanding of the difference between Socialism, Communism & Marxism, also concerning why Socialism is usually disliked where I touched upon the differences between the leader and the ideology being used. In the later chapters, I hope to be able to give more insight concerning Socialism and its vast mysteries that I believe few of you know about. But for now let us take it in, step by step.

II. Freedom VS Overly Restrictive Laws

First Grand Chapter : The Knowledge & Understandings Of Socialism

---

WHICH IDEOLOGY ADVOCATES freedom? Most people will instantly think of Democracy. Which ideology advocates restrictions? People will likely say, authoritative ones. But is freedom a definitely good thing and restrictions a definitely bad thing? If you think about it, not necessarily. When is freedom or restrictions a good thing respectively? I am leaving that to you to ponder upon.

What is the law, and what is it good at doing? The definition of the law is a system of rules that are regulated towards the people in a given country, group, or society where the law is in effect. It is in place as a means to restrict people from forms of misconduct as dictated by lawmakers. This means that every country that has set up laws is restricting its citizens at a societal level. If this is the case, can we truly say that democracy equals freedom if it restricts its people? [A smirk emerges.] Let us continue first before answering this question.

Why do I add the word 'overly' to the title of this chapter? That is because in any country that advocates freedom, lies a system of law that restricts people but the set of laws found in such countries do not exhibit a form of meddling in personal affairs of the individual citizen, in other words, it has restrictions that do not try to invade the life and choices of the individual at a personal level. Whereas ideologies that do not advocate quote-unquote 'freedom' are seen to have laws that directly meddle in the lives of the individual citizen. Coming back to that question, when people say democracy equals freedom, what they usually mean is that the law exists but the laws do not restrict the individual from going about their lives as how they want it to go. More or less, that is the understanding concerning the word 'freedom' within a democracy.

Other than authoritative ideologies, where are overly restrictive laws found that disrupt the personal livelihoods of the people? Surprisingly it is mostly found in religion. For example, the head dressing for Muslims or the head and face coverings that women must wear in the Arab world. Why do they have to wear those coverings? What is the intended purpose? If I may, the reason comes from their perspective that women are beautiful creatures. Men on the other hand are easily tempted by women, hence as a measure to prevent adultery or any form of attraction, women are made to wear these coverings and only open them for their husband's eyes to feast upon. People who do not understand or people who are outside the Muslim world will try to criticize this way of thought that comes from Islam. But to them (to Islam), this is a sacred thing that must be implemented by all Muslim females. I believe this is a form of wisdom from the Muslim world to prevent temptations and acts of impulse from weak-minded men towards uncovered women.

Another example is found in the Christian world, concerning women's rights. When women were fighting for their rights, what was their plea? Women rise up because of abusive husbands and men who belittle them where in some cases women were looked at and treated as objects and not as fellow human beings. But their plea was to be seen as equals with men. (I personally find that their plea was quite strange and different from their problem.) And sadly this plea was granted by a supposedly Christian nation. Why is this a sad thing? Because in the Christian world, God created men to serve God and God created women to be helpers unto the men. If women no longer are committed to being helpers unto the men, therefore the hierarchy that was created through the **wisdom** of God has been altered. This alteration will most likely one day cause men to no longer serve God but may rather cause men to want to be equals with God. Anyway, the restrictive law here was the law whereby women were to be helpers of men and not try to be who they are today; a law that is quite restrictive to how women currently prefer to be.

The last example that I can give you concerning overly restrictive laws, is a form of religious living. Every religion has laws that a good religious person should follow and these laws invade the personal life of the individual. (It may not seem invasive from the point of view of the religious person himself because he wants to do it by his own free will. But usually, it is the outsiders who see it as invasive.) What can be eaten and what cannot be eaten, what words are allowed to be spoken and what words should be avoided, the mandatory yearly celebrations of their religion, and so on. Are these restrictions bad? No, they are not bad. In fact, most of them are derived from words of wisdom. Most of these laws are known to be the wisest thing to do if you want to live a good life in this world or if you want to be closest to God when you go to heaven.

Overly restrictive laws may sound intrusive but every lawmaker creates a law that is based on his own understanding as a means of goodwill. Laws may be seen by outsiders as something bad but from the perspective of the leader, it is something good to have. There is a different understanding at play in most laws. A simple explanation is how a parent understands the reason for having a curfew and how a child sees it as a form of imprisonment or bondage.

As a Socialist myself, I understand that there are laws in Socialism that invade into the personal lives of individuals. But these laws, rules, and regulations are needed for the sake of societal harmony. I am sure that there are people out there who want to control the world and the inhabitants thereof. They will use every means that they can find to reach their goal. But the Socialism that I understand is nothing like the agendas of those people. True Socialists do not want control over the people. What we yearn for is **societal upbringing** and a **societal consciousness** towards it.

There is a saying that goes, "If you listen to the words of a wise man and stick to them without fail, you will inherit his good wishes for you." This is a very good piece of advice. But how do we know that he is a wise man and not a fool? The simple way is to ask the man. For a wise man is willing to impart understanding to those who are likewise willing and have the patience to hear that understanding. Then from there, you discern if whatever he says makes sense to you.

To conclude this chapter, let us do a review. This chapter tells of the difference between laws that govern the people versus laws that invade into the livelihoods of the individual. From my point of view, I have just given you the difference between a society that advocates freedom and a society that advocates harmony induced by wisdom through the placement of overly restrictive laws. **More on this debate later**.

III. Defining Socialism

WHAT IS SOCIALISM exactly? This is a difficult question to answer, considering all the bias information found in books and online searches. I cannot give you a straight answer but I will tell you how Socialism came to be and where this idea is derived from. From there, hopefully, you will be able to deduce, what exactly is Socialism.

I would like to open the mind of the reader to the existence of two different types of people conforming to Socialism or any other ideology for that matter. But firstly, before that, Socialism (or any other ideology) is a set of ideas combined together. Someone must have created the idea in the first place. In fact, all ideologies come from a particular human way of thinking. For example, every rule in Democracy must conform to the same way of thinking. If that is not the case then something is amiss and it shouldn't be called Democracy but rather maybe Democracy with something else added to it. The bottom line is that every rule in an ideology must conform to one single form of thinking. It is from that single form of thinking that all its rules and regulations come from.

Secondly, how a person thinks describes … what? It describes who he is, his actions, his choice of friends, his preferences, his type of girlfriend, and so on. Is it alright for me to say that how a person thinks describes his personality which is shown through his day-to-day character? If we all agree on this, that makes an ideology, not something that consists of rules taken from all over the place but rather from a type of personality and its personal perspective of how life should be like.

The early Socialists were people that have the same personality and with their personality, created the system and ideology known as Socialism. These are the first type of people who conforms to Socialism that is in existence today. Their birth personalities and their personal values conform to Socialism. The second type of people conforming to the ideas of socialism are people who are not born under the star of Socialism but prefer Socialism upon reading about it, and from that day forward, lean towards its ideas and ideals.

Just like how there are 12 constellations and every one of us is born under one of these constellations. To those who believe in this doctrine, they will say that people who are born in the same constellation tend to have the same preferences in life. For example, I was born on august the sixth, this puts me under the star of Leo. But when I read about Virgo, I like Virgo and because of that, I try to be Virgo. My question is, to what extent can I be Virgo? Can I be Virgo 100% and forget about the preferences and behaviors of a Leo? Or if I try to be Virgo when I am originally a Leo, will I end up being something else entirely? This example showcases the second type of people that conforms to an ideology. They are originally born under a specific ideology but they try to conform to a different ideology which may not go hand-in-hand with their unconscious original way of thinking.

Hence the two types of people conforming to an ideology consist of (1) being born with the personality of that ideology and conforming to the ideology that resonates with his birth personality, and (2) being born with an ideology but prefer conforming to a different ideology that does not resonate with his birth personality. This is why we have people who rise under the banner of democracy yet implement socialistic systems, in which case the person may be originally a socialist but because of circumstance or preference, chooses to enter into government under the banner of democracy. There are also instances where the opposite occurs. Because of this understanding, we get a variety of governments that sometimes tend to act against their ideology of choice without knowing it.

One of the examples that I may find in the twenty-first century where democratic government implements socialistic systems is a nationwide health care system where every citizen has to partake in paying a fee per month even though they do not use or care to use that health care system. Is this system wrong? No, it isn't wrong. In fact, it is a good thing for every person to care for their neighbor whether they know the person or not but in some cases the leaders who do this believe that what they implemented are people-friendly democratic systems and they somehow strongly believe it when what they are implementing is actually a socialistic mindset of societal harmony and fellowship. Once again democracy advocates freedom of the individual and by forcing citizens to use a portion of their salary to crowdfund a health care system is not democratic in nature.

Before I go on, I would like the reader to know and understand that many factors come into play when we have a leader or president ruling over a country. (1) The banner he comes to power under, (2) his original way of thinking that may be different from his choice ideology, and lastly (3) his character that may change with time. All these can collide within a person and cause contradictions with whatever goals he has set out in the beginning. He may end up becoming a tyrant, he may become a dictator, he may become a pacifist or he may become the antichrist. But whatever he becomes, an ideology is a set of rules — a way of thought, that does not change with passing time. It is constant. Therefore you may hate the leader but never hate Socialism. Because of the existence of these three things, in every ideology, there exists a multitude of different people who conform to the same ideology. Some of them are one with the ideology but others are in conflict unconsciously. What I am trying to say is that not all who call themselves Socialists are trying to destroy the world. A few are trying their best to build it at the expense of their own life.

1. The First Socialists

EARLY SOCIALISTS WERE not ones that you find in political parties. They had no agenda to take part in elections. They are a group of people who hate competition and will choose not to compete with others to get what they want. With that in mind, the political parties that you see in the twenty-first century, the socialist parties or the social democratic parties, and their other names are what I would not call Socialists. They are a people with the mindset and goal of ushering in Socialism onto a society that already has an existing ideology in place. Forcing Socialism unto the people isn't Socialism, period.

Because you can't find the early Socialists in political parties, where are they found? Early Socialists were community builders. They would find people, advertise their goals to them and together with those who have similar minds, build a society from the ground up. The community that was built were usually closed communities meaning that it shuns itself away from the outside world as a means to have little to do with the outside. These enclosed communities have their own source of food and water. The rule is that everyone has a job to play in the community to support the continual existence thereof.

It is because of this fact that Socialists, have the opposing side which consists of pro-democratic people, telling the world that Socialism imprisons its citizens and prevents them from having choices. This is a misunderstanding. Every enclosed Socialist community, back in the early days, consists of groups of people who choose that form of lifestyle by their own free will. People were not forced or cheated into entering the community. The decision to enter is made by the members of the community themselves and they can also choose to remove themselves from the community without any problems. (People may see that authoritative countries that conform to some type of Socialism do not allow their citizens to remove themselves from the country but let me tell you that originally, Socialism isn't like that.) I want the reader to know that early Socialists have no military power, they have no political power or status. Most of them have no money. (I myself am writing this book in hopes to amass wealth that will then be used to build a socialist city in the twenty-first century.) All they have is a societal mindset and the power of a salesman. They find for like-minded people and build their communities without force or causing fear.

Sadly these enclosed communities were short-lived. Often were they found to last a short while before disbanding totally. If the idea of Socialism was so good, why did this happen? My deductions include : (1) their numbers were small, they had 50 people, 100 at best. (2) The world outside the community was growing at a faster pace than they were. The outside world had people with certain expertise that they didn't have. (3) The inhabitants faced difficulty in interactions between friends and relatives outside the community. (4) Fewer people joined them as time went on. (5) They inevitably got bored due to a lack of all kinds of motivations or life's stimulants that were present in the outside world. They lost interest in the community and went back to the open-world where people can do whatever they want.

The goal of early Socialists was honorable in a sense that they tried to build communities that created a form of societal harmony, bringing people away from the world of wickedness, thefts, competition, unfair practices, joblessness, homelessness, and other worries of that old world. It was a sight we rarely get to see in the characters of modern-day leaders (because somehow there seems like there is an unseen force restricting their movements from doing more good towards the people just as how a good **King** could; It saddens me personally to see good leaders being bound by the laws of the country, which disables them to help and serve the people better).

2. Transitions From Socialism To Communism

SOCIALISM, which tried to bring about societal harmony, did not stay for very long. But the fire of Socialism didn't stop there. People still believed if only socialist communities had more people in them and the people had more things that can be done in them, it would exist for longer periods of time.

As the world continues and capitalism surfaced, competitions between companies grow rampant and inequalities start to appear at a massive scale. Workers were paid lesser and lesser. People were fighting for a day's wages. Capitalism plays a great role in the prolonged existence of Socialism. For those who are wondering what is capitalism, in simple terms: it is the allowing of competition between businesses, all for the goal of self-profit.

How does a businessman make more profit? By lowering the wages of the workers, the goods sold by the business can be sold at fewer costs hence compete against other similar businesses and by winning the market, be able to eradicate the competition at the same time but at the expense of hurting the factory workers who are trying to make a living.

The only ideology in existence that was against self-profit was Socialism. Democracy was never against self-profit because it allowed the freedom of the individual to hoard money for themselves despite its repercussions towards any parties involved. The people affected by this were hoping for a change to be presented to them by their leaders but the leaders governed by democratic values were unable to do anything about this issue.

Because the damage done by the rise of Capitalism was nationwide, Socialists needed a way to quell the problem at a national level. This is when they started entering into politics and forming political parties in order to win votes and bring about a socialist revolution. But a revolution was never the intended goal of Socialism, therefore, those who choose the path of enforcing Socialism unto a people because of their strong beliefs in the salvation of Socialism, broke away from Socialism and became known as Communism which is the means of forcing Socialism unto a society of people where exists a resistance towards Socialism itself.

What resistance am I referring to? During an election, we usually end up seeing two parties, one with a larger percentage of the votes, the other with a fewer percentage of the votes. The resistance is the fewer percentage of the votes. A presidential election with a sixty percent win means you have a forty percent resistance. **Socialism** hates competition and **does not enter** into a political competition because **it must have** 100% support from the people for it **to exist without fail**. Therefore Socialists choose to build up communities with the same mindset from the ground up. But because Communism is Socialism with the addition of using force, when Communists win an election with a percentage of resistance, they tend to be forceful towards the resistance because of their roots in Socialism which **needs** that 100% support from the whole community. This gives the understanding why most of the time Communism is strict towards the people and shows a form of authoritarianism or dictatorships that may turn into violence that violates human rights or even go to the extent of genocide. Communism needs that 100% full support of the people and this is what happens when you force Socialism because of the resistance found in the people who do not want to conform to Socialism.

Now you know that Communism comes from Socialism but the path it chooses to take in order to bring about Socialism is by means of force. **True Socialism**, on the other hand, does not apply force because it needs the understanding of every individual to **willingly accept** its ideology (and the values thereof) in order to move forward together as a big community, and by going at it this way, it will **always get** 100% support of the society (because once again, everyone in society willingly chooses, out of a form of societal wisdom, to live this way).

3. Communism & Marxism

WHEN WE TALK about Marxism, we are talking about the mind of a man by the name of Karl Marx and his intellectual findings. Who is Karl Marx? He is the author of the book called 'the Communist Manifesto' which dictates how Communism should be and how it can be achieved.

I have previously stated what an ideology is, which is a way of thought based on the personality of the person. But there is also something else that can bring about a change of mindset in how a person thinks and that is a person's religious views and how strongly his beliefs are.

You can read all about Karl Marx when you search about him but briefly, Karl Marx is a logical-thinking, fact-finding human being. He was an intelligent man who likes to read and has much knowledge. His writings will tell you that he has amass understandings of the workings of society. If you do search about Marxism, you will find out that this ideology impacted some of the minds of great people in the past, two of which are Joseph Stalin and Mao Zedong.

Although he is such a marvelous person depicted in online searches, as a Socialist, I personally do not see eye to eye with him about a couple of things that I find important to the growth and well-being of society. Most of these things come from Karl's strong religious belief in atheism.

Because he is an atheist, this makes him a hardworking person who lives by logical means — facts. Because he does not lean on any form of God but rather lean on himself to achieve anything at all, he burdens himself with life. His writings are based on diligent studies of the economy and market systems. The goal of this intellectual being was to create a classless society for humankind in such a way that equality and fairness become a reality in society.

If we were to speak about the goal of Karl Marx, there is nothing wrong about his love for societal harmony. In fact, we all love a good man who is trying his best by using his brain to create the blueprint of a society where the rich does not control the poor because those two groups do not exist — every person is at the same class level, to be treated equally by the system that governs society. But if there is one thing that I dislike about this man, that would be that he is an intellectual atheist who fills his writings with atheistic values.

An atheist is surely not a man of faith but rather a man who leans on his own understanding of things. This gives people with strong atheistic views an ability to critically analyze information and with their logical understandings come up with solutions and results that are accurate most of the time. There is nothing wrong with this. But when you put together the character of an atheist and the character of a good man trying to provide a form of well-being to society, we end up with a problem rising up towards societies that have various religions.

Karl Marx is a man who is called the father of Communism. This does not mean that he created Communism as how other narratives confirm it to be. But Communism itself was present before he was even born. Karl Marx was a believer of Communism, he believed that Socialism can only be achieved by means of a revolution that is ignited from the working-class people. His detailed writings of 'how to achieve Communism' gave him that title.

Karl Marx has the same heart as that of a Communist. And the goal of Communism is the same as Socialism but with the application of force added to it. Because Socialism wants to bring about societal harmony, so too is the agenda of Karl Marx but in the terms of Karl Marx, it is to bring about a 'classless society' where everyone is on the same level and the terms 'rich' & 'poor' do not exist. This is a noble thing to do for human civilization but the only problem I have with this man is that he has a strong atheistic belief.

Let me give you a case scenario. I am a Christian and I am in love with a Muslim female. If I have strong Christian views and I love her, I would want her to go to the same heaven as I do when death comes to take her, yes? Will I want that for her? Yes, I would. Because I believe that my religion is true while her religion is false therefore through the notion of quote-unquote 'goodwill' I invite her over to Christianity. My two traits are (1) I am a Christian, (2) I have goodwill based on my religion.

The goodwill of Socialism is to bring about societal harmony. The goodwill of Communism is to bring about societal harmony for all, through the use of force. The goodwill of Marxism is to bring about the societal harmony known as a classless society. If Communism is actually Socialism plus force, and Marxism came from the thinking of Communism, therefore Marxism has (1) Goodwill, (2) It showcases the application of revolutionary force, (3) it conforms to atheistic beliefs.

What is religion to strong-minded atheists? There are atheists in this world who are neutral when the topic of God comes to mind. But radical atheists believe that religion is nothing. They understand that logical thinking is something but faith is nothing. Karl Marx is not only an atheist but he openly rejects and hates religion. His hatred towards religion embodies him in such a way that his writings are critical towards the idea of allowing religion to exist. According to him, religion must be eradicated in order to advance, if not, one day when we no longer are around, religion will cause the downfall of everything we have tried to achieve for the sake of human civilization.

If the goodwill of a Christian is to bring people into Christianity, what is the goodwill of radical atheists who wants to help society move forward? I presume that they would be telling people, "Hey, forget your religion. Come, I will help you out with whatever you need and you can see for yourself that everything can be done and achieved by societal means if we all just come together and help each other out."

Karl Marx wanted the people to be independent of any form of God. This is to give the understanding that a man can only live by the force of himself. It is by means of the will of self that we achieve anything at all. This is his understanding, the mindset of atheism. (It is also with this mindset, that leaders who idolize Marxism end up persecuting religion — because Karl Marx, the founder of Marxism hated religion which he dictated in his writings, be it consciously or unconsciously.)

In the case of Marxism, they will not kindly ask you to join in with their way of thinking but they will make sure that you do what they say. This is the problem that I have against Marxism — an anti-religious form of Socialism.

I see Karl Marx as a man with goodwill for the sake of human civilization and its future existence thereof. I believe Karl Marx sees himself also as a good man trying to do good to our civilization by means of his own understanding as an intellectual being who has studied papers and books and use all the information he has accumulated to devise a way forward. The problem is that an atheist with goodwill towards mankind will end up trying to free mankind from their delusions of religion because to them God is nonexistent. The only thing existing in this world, according to radical atheists, is the person and that person's hard work and diligence. Religion is seen as a hindrance to societal growth with regard to medicine or technology, hence ultimately restricting the advancement of human civilization. Do not forget that Marxism also applies force. This is why we have countries whose government conforms to Marxism, currently cracking down on all forms of religion.

Marxism is an idea from Karl Marx who strongly hates religion and this causes an impact on its view about any religion. His writings, although hope to bring about societal harmony in his own terms, are heavily intertwined with his atheistic beliefs and so hope to bring about a future where religion is abolished. It is with this knowledge that every person who conforms to Marxism will inevitably do the same.

4. The Siblings Of Socialism

I VIEW SOCIALISM as how it came to be originally. But there are intellectual people who define Socialism or Early Socialists, as being utopian dreamers — naive thinkers. To them (intellectual people), they believe that Socialism is an ideology that already implies the use of force otherwise it is just a dream.

Intellectual beings in the world today, because of the popular writings and definitions of Karl Marx, view Socialism through the spectacles of Karl Marx. Whatever

Socialism is, is understood as whatever Karl Marx sees it to be.

According to the history of the world, there are 4 groups of people who conform to the way of Socialism. (1) The First Socialists who are, through the eyes of modern Socialists, nonexistent. (2) The Socialists who enter into political parties, mingling with democracy to form a hybrid form of Socialism. (3) Revolutionary Socialists which are commonly known as Communists. And (4) Marxists, those who conform to the writings of Karl Marx.

But from my point of view, there are only 3 types of Socialism. (1) Socialism, (2) Communism, and (3) Marxism. These 3 siblings have similar goals but how they plan on executing their plans to achieve those goals is what makes them different.

Socialism is the first ideology that tries to bring about societal harmony which comes from the need for equality. Because of the failures of Socialism, Communism came into existence. And because of the difficulties in the implementation of Communism, Marxism came into existence. This makes Communism a form of Socialism that tries to succeed where Socialism failed and makes Marxism a form of Communism that tries to succeed where Communism failed.

We know that Communism enforces its ideology unto the people, a form of revolutionary Socialism. Socialism itself was never revolutionary and was never imposed onto the people. Therefore having seen the fall of socialism, communism tried to do what socialism never did. As for marxism, seeing how communism has difficulties implementing itself, chooses the way of a clever & cunning approach. The goals are similar but the process by which they each try to reach their goals is different. But the reader must know that the process by which the result is achieved has a big impact on the result itself, once it has been achieved.

Socialism is the eldest brother, wise and gentle.
Communism is the second brother, impatient and brutal.
Marxism is the youngest brother, intelligent and cunning.

(Therefore if you see a leader who idolizes Marxism, you have to be very cautious and very prepared because the technique of Marxism is a high form of cleverness. And when you are facing someone who is very clever, who knows that he cannot win with force, openly or directly as shown in the failures of revolutionary Socialism, he will use **subtle** and **indirect** ways to accomplish whatever he has set out to do, which is the most dangerous opponent to be facing against.)

Let me recap what these 3 siblings did. Socialism tried to build societies from scratch which ended up in failure because of the 5 reasons that I have mentioned previously. Communism tried to enter into politics in order to win votes so that they could enter into societies and implement

Socialism to the whole country in hopes that they do not end up in the same failure as the small communities of Socialism. Because communism was revolutionary in their cause and often causes havoc, they were met with much resistance from people of power and status who didn't like their idea. Then came the cunning brother who chooses to use subtleness and intrigue to pave his way into success.

Warning : Marxist governments currently are trying to subdue the world using the same technique they managed to get into governments. The world must take note of this issue. The reason Marxist governments seem to try to rule the world is because of the writings of Karl Marx himself. In order for the evils of capitalism to be abolished from the world, Marxist governments need to have some form of control over the economies of the world. By doing this, the home countries of the Marxist governments will be safe and protected from the evils of capitalism that can be directed to them through trade between countries.

When Socialism build communities from scratch, their goal was to keep capitalism from ever entering into their societies. When Communism wanted to force Socialism upon a country, their goal was to abolish capitalism from the country totally. When a country is already being led by a Marxist ideology, the next step is to ensure that their country will never come face to face with another country that wants to do bad unto them. Therefore as a means to protect themselves, the **defense mechanism** of a Marxist is to have some form of economic control over the world economy.

IV. Capitalism, The Basic Enemy Of Socialism

First Grand Chapter : The Knowledge & Understandings Of Socialism

---

THE FORMAL DEFINITION of Capitalism is that it is a system in which a country's trade and industry are controlled by private owners rather than the state or government. In other words, capitalism allows people to be able to own businesses. In Capitalism, people are allowed to open their own restaurants, massage parlors, barbershops, supermarkets, transportation services, and so on, where all these businesses can be set up by the people and earn big profits through their trade. This allows employment of the masses but on the **terms** of the employer.

What do I mean by 'on the terms of the employer'? This is what it means. The employer can choose to hire people and set their wages to be whatever amount they want. Of course, people can negotiate the salary but it all comes down to the employer. The employer can also terminate the employee based on the signed document that the employee must sign before joining the establishment. The goal of the government is to serve the well-being of the people. But the goal of business owners is to make a profit. To allow Capitalism is to give the people over to be stepped upon by corporate interests.

Because of Capitalism, companies doing the same trade as one another, compete for the market. This in turn causes hurt towards the employees of both the winning side and the losing side. We the consumers are happy to purchase low-cost goods but behind the scenes, people are losing jobs, children of those families are affected. To fight off Capitalism, which is one of the major parts of all Democracies, democratic governments set up government-owned schools and other government-owned services to help out with the damage Capitalism does incur unto working-class families.

We all have witnessed in our lives that there exist both good and bad people. But when it comes down to Capitalism and the workings of businesses, there are more bad than good in them because what people tend to chase after is profit, neglecting the health and problems that their employees may have because of the respective jobs being undertaken.

What Socialism tries to tackle is the evil and wicked people of the world. Therefore we are authoritative when setting rules, to prevent wicked hearts from surfacing in society. Wicked people are people who have bad intentions and bad motives toward their fellow human beings. By creating restrictive laws, even unto invading the personal life of the individual, this we do to secure the well-being of every other individual. This is the basic nature of Socialists, that is to save people from what we deemed may cause future societal breakdowns. Therefore how we think and the way we think must be in a good way that is acceptable to the people, if not it will show in our actions towards the people as something bad. This is the reason as I have stated before that the way of the early Socialists (which is the building of society from scratch and then calling out people into the society to live with us) is the only way for Socialism. Socialism should never be imposed upon the people that do not want it in the first place. Socialism is similar to religion in a sense where Heaven is built for a people with a particular mindset to live in it — those who choose Godliness (which is a life of various restrictions) willingly will tend to be given the keys unto heaven but those who do not choose Godliness, will find themselves not allowed to enter because it doesn't fit their lifestyle of choice.

Back to Capitalism. Capitalism is a major part of democratic values — a freedom to do business that will not be intervened by the state or government at a personal level. Socialism and all its other direct siblings are more anti-capitalism than we are anti-democracy. We who are pro-people with regard to livelihoods and well-beings of the individual, try our best to find ways to build a world where capitalism does not prosper.

From a capitalist standpoint, they tend to resist Socialism and any form of government that tries to take their factories and businesses from them. I believe it is the right of any business owner to take this same resisting stance. Therefore true Socialists don't want to have anything to do with these people. We block them out when we create our societies. But in most cases, it is these people that end up entering into our societies and trying to build businesses in Socialistic environments. And when we say no to them, they say we are the bad guys. In fact, the world sees Socialism as a bad ideology because most branded media outlets are owned by businessmen.

I believe that everyone may have an entrepreneur mindset but if the mindset can be molded in such a way that it benefits the whole society, we Socialists are open to working with people of that nature but not with people seeking self-profit. As a matter of fact, Socialists are great business thinkers but we plan our economic systems for the sake of the community as a whole, and not just to please some group of people.

I see a future where even though societies do end up conforming to Socialism, there will always be a sense of wanting to own a business coming from the citizens. This is because there exists in the human character to want to be better than others, to want to have more than others, to want to be different from others. People feel an accomplishment when they thrive over others. If we cannot change the mindset of the people to yearn for collective societies where we do everything for the existence of the society, there will be no way of stopping the cycles of history from repeating itself.

V. Addressing Critics Towards Socialism

THERE EXIST GROUPS of people with various backgrounds that love to critic the ways and mindset of Socialists. These are the few that I have found.

1. Socialism Practices A Form Of Slavery

CRITICS BELIEVE THAT Socialism wants the people to rely on the state so that the people will not know what independent success is and because of that, end up creating a people who unconsciously are enslaved by the state because, without the state, they will not know how to live. In other words, Socialism to them is trying to imprison people in such a way that the people lose their will towards being independent. I believe this is the same way how Atheists see people within religion; they see them as being imprisoned by religion itself, and they want to free them from it.

This is not totally nonsense. There will always exist people who use the word Socialism to control people. But when I first heard about it, I was angered at their perspective. The success of a Socialist society is a collective success — a success meant to be experienced by the whole community. A caring Socialist leader serves the people and does not make profits for himself. That being said, bad intentions were never found in the way of thinking of a caring Socialist leader. It may just seem so or look as though whatever the critics say are true, analyzed by those who have eyes to see, but there isn't any intention to enslave the people, at least not when the reigns are being held by true Socialists who conform to the early Socialists' mindset.

As a matter of fact, real slavery is found to be done by regular citizens within the walls of Democracy. And not just slavery, but also prostitution, forcing drugs on others, and abuse are also being done by regular citizens towards other regular citizens within Democracy. The problem within Democracy is that you give people the freedom to not just do good to their fellow citizens but also do bad to anyone out there and the ideology of Democracy itself does not do anything to stop this despicable character coming from human beings because Democracy finds it wrong to be overly restrictive in its societies. Well done Democracy! You allow Freedom but your people end up losing fairness and justice because of that freedom.

2. Socialism Thinks It Can Print Money Without Causing Inflation

THIS IS ONE of the most misunderstood principles of Socialism. Some have tried to blindly follow this principle of Socialism and end up in failure. This then of course is used by intellectuals to further mock the understanding of printing money out of thin air. From my understanding, I believe we can print money out of thin air. In fact, there is a way that you can print money without causing inflation but there must be some conditions that have to be met first. I will not disclose to the reader here how we Socialists are correct in this matter but if you keep reading, you will come across our intended meaning — a mindset only from the minds of early Socialists.

3. Socialism Is As Good As Its Writer, Karl Marx

I SEE THIS as an insult to Socialism. Karl Marx didn't invent Socialism. He understands Socialism and defines what Socialism is in his writings. People who read his writings end up seeing Socialism through **his spectacles**. And to tell you the truth, his writings, because of their detailed explanation and precise choice of words used, his writings were popular during that time. Therefore everyone's understanding of definitions and principles about Socialism and other related stuff came from his understanding of how the world is. In other words, people at that time **preferred his definition** of things compared to the writings of other writers which wasn't as good as his. This played a big role in the current world's understanding towards Socialism — some intellectuals see him as the creator of Socialism, because of that past popularity in his writings that still defines Socialism to this day.

I see intellectual critics as people who like reading books — that's how they brand themselves intellectuals. The reader must understand that most writings found today about Socialism and its principles came from the famous best-selling writings of one man, and that is Karl Marx. Therefore anyone who tries to redefine what Socialism is —

gets kicked out of the picture. Although people hate Karl Marx, unbeknownst to the modern intellectuals themselves, they are using his understanding of what Socialism is and all other economic definitions used by the world are mostly based on his writings. I believe I have previously written an unpublished article about this. Allow me to copy and paste it as additional content for this topic if I can just find it, if not there will be nothing left to add.

4. Socialism Will Eventually Lead To Communism

THIS UNDERSTANDING IS also based on the writings of Karl Marx. Karl Marx sees Communism as Socialism version 2.0 which is not true. This is only found in the mindset of Karl Marx and his followers who include the intellectuals who read his book and conforms to his writings.

On one side we have Socialism, which is patient and does not force its ideals of societal existence onto the people. And then we have Communism, which is hasty and does indeed force the ideals of Socialism unto the people.

Socialism and Communism are likened to the words, loving care & conditional love. Loving care can be done one-sided but conditional love needs the two-way. If a man falls in love with a woman and the woman rejects him, when he gets angry because of the rejection he received, which love did he have towards her? Is it the loving care type of love or the conditional type of love? When you have loving care towards a person and that person rejects you, you still care for that person while you find for someone else. But if you have conditional love, people tend to hate the person when they get rejected. This is why Communism does not go well with resistance and upon meeting resistance turns authoritative towards that resistance. Whereas Socialism takes a different stance and either relocates itself or the resistance somewhere else but still is open if that resistance wants to change.

What Communism does is that it believes it is doing something good to society. (Actually, people conforming to any ideologies believe that they are doing something good to society.) But to Communists, because they believe they do something good to the society, they want and yearn for the whole support of the society because of their goodwill. Just like a husband who do all things for his wife and because he asks her to sleep with him one night but she refuses (because he previously did something bad to one of her family members) and they end up fighting because the man believes he has done his utmost goodwill to the family but the wife doesn't want to support him. Communism is something like this.

Socialism like other ideologies also believe it is doing something good to society and when the people don't want to follow, we reason with them and the worst-case scenario would be that those good believers of Socialism will relocate them somewhere else with financial compensation depending on their previous contributions to our collective society. Socialism will accommodate them the best we can and not ask anything in return but rather provision them as we send them off. Either that or strike a deal with them through an everlasting contract of sorts where they do not disturb us and we will not disturb them. Bottom line is that Socialism gives a choice to the people, "Work with us and together we will make happy the society we live in, if not we will find someone else who is willing to care for their fellow neighbor as themselves but still be open to help you in any way we can if you one day need help."

Socialism will be sad to see you go yet still be caring towards you. But Communism will be angry when you decide to go and will hate you and probably force you to stay or get abusive.

I hope that the reader gets the picture. Socialism and Communism are two different things yet somehow Karl Marx explains it in the narrative of Capitalism failing which turns into Socialism and from Socialism transits into Communism. He uses an economic narrative to define the inevitable transition between Capitalism to Communism by firstly going through Socialism. Whereas he forgets that Socialism is not just an economic theory for wealth management and distribution but it is also a philosophical understanding of societal existential & continuous existence founded by early Socialists. Because Karl Marx sees early Socialists as naive thinkers and builders of a dreamlike society, therefore he probably didn't consider their mindset worthy of being understood.

5. The Globalist Agenda Is A Socialist Agenda

To ME, this is an interesting statement. First of all, what is a Globalist? A Globalist is someone who likes the idea of a controlled society where society can be manipulated to usher in what the Globalists believe is an ideal society. In other words, they want the people to unconsciously build a world to the liking of the Globalists themselves. Also, this implies that the people unknowingly are manipulated to change the world into what the Globalists want the world to be like. So the Globalists want to build a society where they can live good lives but they do so by means of subtly controlling the world into building that world for them.

Globalists may seem to have a Socialist form of thinking but from the previous paragraph, the reader may understand that Globalism is a selfish form of Marxism. Marxism wants to usher in a world where every person is equal, using its methods of intrigue, whereas, Globalism wants to achieve an ideal society not necessarily for every person in the world but rather for themselves to live in and they use the people to achieve their goals. Marxism's focus is the people but the focus of Globalists are themselves.

The way I see it, Globalists are actually Capitalists using Marxist theories to secure their future way of living.

A very short conclusion. The globalist agenda is not a Socialist agenda or a Communist one or even a Marxist agenda because the agenda of the three respectively, is not a selfish agenda, but rather all 3 brothers focus on the sake of the people. Communism may be brutal but it is not selfish. Marxism may want to persecute religion but it isn't selfish either. Socialism, Communism & Marxism, do all that they can for the better good of the people with regard to their respective mindsets. But Globalism, on the other hand, does all it can for the better good of itself.

6. Socialism, An Ideology that God Detests

THIS STATEMENT COMES from the mouth of intellectual people in the religious world. Christian pastors hate Socialism which causes also the Christian congregations to hate Socialism. We may also have other religions hating Socialism but I am only informed of Christianity being the only religion that dislikes Socialism.

First things first. As I have mentioned previously, the reader must know what Socialism is. It isn't Communism, it isn't Marxism and it isn't Globalism. So what can a person hate about Socialism if it is separated from the other three mentioned ideologies? People hate Socialism because they believe it is one of those three mentioned ideologies. But if I tell them that it isn't, will they still hate Socialism?

Because I believe they will, let me enlighten the religious world towards the similarities of Socialism and the Godly realm.

1) The early Socialists, build societies to fend off evil people — those who have wickedness in their hearts to rob their fellow brothers and sisters.

2) Early Socialists teach the sharing of thy property with the collective people in its society.

3) The people in Socialist societies are to show care and love for their neighbors.

4) Food is presented by the collective to every worker within Socialist societies as a form of thanks for their participation within society.

5) Socialism asks and needs the people to conform to the understanding of the laws and regulations within, which is good for the sake of a form of goodwill to be done from one citizen unto other fellow citizens.

"Of all these statements that I give to you, which ones do you find unacceptable to religion? The following points below represent the Godly realm."

1) Evil people and those with evil intentions are hated by God.

2) A Godly community is one where we share what we have with the people living with us.

3) Love and care are found in religious people. Every person who is really religious does this thing.

4) Those who do not want to work, should not eat.

5) God says that one day, the people will live by His statutes and His laws will be found in the hearts of His people who conform to His being and values. By doing so, the people in the kingdom will never be

oppressed by the people of God but rather harmony will be within its gates.

"Do you see the similarities now?"

Although the similarities are seen, people will still say that the Socialism that I presented is different from the workings of a Godly Kingdom. Yes, as a Christian myself, I believe that no matter how good I build up a city for the people to live in, it would not compare to the kingdom where God is the leader thereof. The only thing that I could highlight is that a leader will always want to ensure that the people conform to the leader's values and understanding. Now, if the leader is a good person, the values that become laws and regulations within the city, will be heavily based on his being and wisdom. And if that good leader is a King, what more good impact it will have on society because a King is above the law and a good King will be a good lawmaker.

VI. Brief Conclusion Of Grand Chapter : Socialism

FIRST GRAND CHAPTER : THE KNOWLEDGE &
UNDERSTANDINGS OF SOCIALISM

THE IDEOLOGY OF Socialism consists of a set of ideas and ideals that yearn for the well-being of society that hopes to bring about a harmonious continuous existence of a society that is rid of known problems and is rid of the characteristics of human beings that may intend on harming the society.

The direct siblings of Socialism are Communism and Marxism. They are known as the direct siblings because of their similar idea as with Socialism that was in existence before both of them ever came into being. The idea of Communism came from Socialism with forceful actions added to the idea of Socialism. The idea of Marxism came from Communism but with added meticulous planning to achieving it. All three have the same goal of helping out people in a way that class hierarchies disappear to create a one-level social class status for all the people where everyone is seen as equals with one another, doing their respective jobs for the continual existence of the whole society.

The Cousins of Socialism are those who try to mix other ideologies with Socialism with a goal towards the well-being of society which includes the social-democratic people. The enemy of Socialism is Capitalism. The half-cousins of Socialism are the people who are being called the Globalists; these are the ones who I believe are Capitalists that are using the trickeries of Marxism to reach their selfish agenda that does not prioritize the well-being of the people.

We also talked about an ideology (a set of ideas and ideals) being based on a mindset (a way of thinking) and how that ideology is presented unto the people is based on the character of the leader, his views about life — the justice within his personality; which together with his being, embodies the leader to lead the people forward according to how he sees well to do unto the people, towards a goal that is derived from his will, which may not in particularly conform 100% to the ideology he, came into power with, or, currently holds the view of.

Overall, although Communism & Marxism may seem like modern forms of Socialism, they are not. But rather all three have different processes by which they intend on reaching their goal of continual societal existence in harmony. And remember, anything and everything can affect the mind of the leader that makes a change towards how he leads.

There is a big difference between the character of the leader with the ideals found within the ideology that he chooses to lead with, not necessarily are they the same.

Once again (hopefully for the last time), **in theory**, Socialism and its direct siblings hope to do good for the sake of the whole society. But **in practice**, it may be different caused by (1) the process by which the ideology used tends on reaching that goal (Communism = forced, Marxism = forced & meticulous planning which include subtle and actions of intrigue), & (2) depends on the will of the leader leading the country, which also includes his personal viewpoints and other factors, that may cause him to **derail from** the theory and the original understanding of the ideology.

This makes Socialism to be without fault in the case of a bad Socialist dictator showing up and doing evil things towards its people. **But** because Communism uses force, therefore a forceful leader under Communism or Marxism, is not morally wrong according to the two ideologies respectively — they can be seen as bad people from the outside world, but they do not derail from their choice ideology, which does indeed need to show force. And therefore, the moment a democratic leader **derails from** the ideals of Democracy, no longer does he conform to Democracy 100%. A leader's personal values (eg. religion or beliefs or viewpoints or philosophy of life or understanding of things or personality or character, etc.) will always play a part in how he rules the people, period.

Supportive Definition References : Their Meanings & Information

Preferring Socialism Over Democracy : Envisioning Cities Of Societal Harmony & Continual Coexistence

---

THIS SECTION IS filled with definitions that will support the understanding of other concepts used within this book.

I. Defining Paper Money

Supportive Definition References : Their Meanings & Information

---

I ONCE ASKED a question. What is money in terms of notes that we use to purchase things? The answer was that these notes act as a representation to something of value.

The following is an exemplar scenario. There is an island that has 1000 people on it and turning the whole wealth of the island into gold coins would give the 1000 people a sum of 100,000 gold coins to share amongst themselves. When they decided to share it equally, each person gets 100 gold coins to live and do business with one another. These people saw that using gold coins to buy food is wasteful because, with one gold coin, they would buy food, and before that one person could finish the food, 97% of the food they bought turns rotten in due time. This causes them to share food with their neighbors so that food is not wasted. But the one who shares the food started complaining because he is the one that has to use his gold coin and these people who eat the food bought by his gold coin do not repay him back. So because gold coins cannot be halved, they created a system of only dollars without cents. These dollars are represented by paper notes. $1, $2, $5, $10, $20, $50, $100, $200 and $500 paper notes were created. In conclusion, one gold coin gives them $10,000 meaning that the whole wealth of the country is valued at $1,000,000,000, which follows the calculation of the number of gold coins multiplied by the fixed value of each gold coin also assuming the gold coins do not change in value over time.

These paper notes represent the wealth of the country which is 100,000 gold coins. And these gold coins were placed in a vault. Let's assume these are honest people and they would not steal from another person. Twenty years passed and they had children amongst themselves, increasing their population by 300 hence their total population becomes 1,300 people. But that does not mean the wealth of the country increases. The **value of** wealth in this new society stays $1,000,000,000 in paper notes represented by the 100,000 gold coins. To increase the countries' wealth, the logical way is to find new gold coins to be placed into their vaults, hence increasing their wealth by the value that was put into their vaults.

In this scenario, imagine that there are seven other islands whose population ranges from 1000 to 1800 people but with exactly the same wealth of 100,000 in gold coins and using the same currency of dollars hence also having $1,000,000,000 to represent their respective 100,000 gold coins. Meaning that the total wealth the 8 islands have together is 800,000 in gold coins. Now if they do not increase their wealth but decided to trade amongst their islands, whatever happens, whether a country gets their amounts of dollars increased or decreased, due to the trade, the total wealth of the eight islands will stay as 800,000 in gold coins or \$8,000,000,000 in dollars. This is the idea of having gold in the vaults and issuing money to represent the gold that each island has. None of these 2 things increases over time.

From the above example, we could see how the wealth of a country is represented in paper notes. If a person catches 50 fishes in the example above, that does not mean that the wealth of the eight islands become \$8,000,000,000 + 50 fishes. Because if he sells the 50 fishes, he gets a sum of paper notes in return from the people he sells them to.

If we use this example in countries in this time and age, it will only be okay if paper money is printed out as the wealth (number of gold coins) of the country increases. But why are there countries printing out paper money without firstly increasing the countries' wealth? When they print the paper money from wealth that does not exist, where do they get it from? Because if we use the \$8,000,000,000 from the example above, and a country decided to print \$100,000,000 more in paper money, they need to get the wealth from somewhere right? This is where the next topic of discussion comes into play. But let us recap what we now know first. Paper money is not wealth but rather it represents the value of a country's wealth broken up into small bills. The technical term for it is banknotes. In modern society, it is supposedly the country's central bank that keeps the wealth itself (in the example above being gold coins). These are the ones that print your money.

II. Defining Inflation

A STONE DOES not rise in worth over time. Its mass also remains the same. But what the world sees when the price of gold rises every day is actually an illusion that can be explained.

Let me give you an explanation based on the story I gave in 'Defining Paper Money' where I say that paper money is represented by gold coins stored in vaults.

This is what happens during inflation. Because the vaults of gold coins are owned by the island as a collective (as a whole community), therefore it is the governing body that ends up being in charge of it. Paper money is printed by the government body in the first place to equal the value of gold coins in the vaults. Paper money in this case becomes a form of medium, that substitutes the gold coins, in order to purchase goods. Because of businesses and the unintentional hoardings of paper money over time by the people who own big flourishing businesses, paper money becomes scarce to the public. When paper money becomes scarce to the public, because paper money is needed to buy goods or services in order to give work to workers, jobs are lost because paper money no longer circulates within the society but rather kept in the houses of employers. When jobs are lost, people end up not being able to have enough paper money to make a purchase to feed themselves. In a case like this, the government body ends up quelling the problem.

How does the government quell the problem for the lack of paper money circulating the society which causes (1) the loss of jobs because of fewer people buying goods and services, and (2) lesser people buying goods and services because of the lack of paper money? They do it by simply printing more paper money that is already in existence and then choose to either give it as a one-time stipend to its citizens or create new jobs for the citizens to do and then pay the citizens for doing the job, with the new paper money that was printed.

Previously, an island has 100,000 gold coins which are represented by 1 billion dollars in paper notes. When the government prints an extra 250 million dollars in paper notes and give them to the people in whichever way he decides to use, now this makes the 100,000 gold coins no longer be represented by 1 billion dollars in paper notes but rather be represented by 1.25 billion dollars in paper notes. When this happens the value of a $1 paper note after the printing of the 250 million dollars, retains its original value by the following percentage : (1000 million / 250 million + 1000 million) = 0.8 which is 80%. Therefore when a donut cost $2 previously, after the printing of the 250 million dollars (a quarter of the previous amount in existence) into the island's economy, the cost of a donut becomes : ($2 / 0.8) = $2.5

Inflation makes it look like the value of goods and services rises by a percentage but what actually happens is not the value that rises but the amount of paper money required to purchase the same goods and services increases. Previously I only need $2 of paper-money-amount to purchase a donut. But now I need $2.5 of paper-money-amount to purchase a donut. The value of the donut with regard to gold coins stays the same. Previously, a donut costs 0.0002 of a gold coin. After the inflation, a donut still cost 0.0002 of a gold coin. The gold coins in the vaults do not increase in numbers. The current number of total gold coins still is 100,000 gold coins in the vaults. Now, the representation of a gold coin previously was 1 gold coin = $10,000. But after inflation, a gold coin is represented by $12,500. Before a donut costs 0.0002 * $10,000 = $2. After inflation, a donut costs 0.0002 * $12,500 = $2.5. The value of the donut does not change, only the amount of paper money nominal is increased.

This inflation that is done by the government body is to fight against hoarders of paper money. As I have explained previously, in most cases it is by unintentional means that an employer hoards paper money because of his booming business. A man feeds one mouth. If he has a family, he feeds

2 to 5 mouths. As for the rest of his earnings, he ends up storing it in his house, because he does not use it. When a business flourishes, the employer ends up getting a lot of excess paper money that he does not need. Although the next topic of definition is '**Defining Paper Money - Part 2**' which talks about money being a medium of exchange, I have to stress out over here that paper money was not meant to be kept and hoarded because it is a means for everyone to buy goods and services. But these flourishing businesses, end up hoarding paper money (probably most of the time) without (a form of intended) evil intentions and (also) without the knowledge of what paper money is exactly, and so they just let it be.

Every time the government body does inflation, it is because of 2 main causes, (1) the government needs instant money for its projects, or (2) to quell the loss of job crisis in society that comes from the scarcity of paper money in circulation. Good governments work with private banks to know the amount of paper money left in circulation by knowing how much is currently being stored in banks nationwide. Bad governments tend to use inflation when they need instant money. I use the word 'bad governments' because there are other better means to get funding other than causing inflation.

The bottom line about inflation is that inflation (1) is the increase of paper money amount that originally represented, in the case of the islands, gold coins — a form of value. Inflation (2) causes the illusion that goods rise in value when in fact it is the paper money that loses value. Inflation (3) is used by good governments to help society by creating new money at the expense of those who keep excess paper money that is accumulated in numbers every month. This is a good point that I would like to expand upon. When a government does inflation unto its country's economy, it indirectly takes a percentage of the value of paper money being held by all people nationwide to create new money that represents the exact percentage taken from those people with savings or a form of savings. This derives the understanding that another definition of savings can be known as 'withheld paper money' — paper money that is held unto or excess paper money that is unused. Inflation (4) has a bigger effect on everyone who has savings in the form of paper money, than those who do not have savings in the form of paper money. Inflation still hurts both parties but it tends to hurt more the people who withheld paper money in their bank accounts or store them in their houses because paper money loses value during inflation.

III. Defining Paper Money - Part 2

SUPPORTIVE DEFINITION REFERENCES : THEIR
MEANINGS & INFORMATION

IN DEFINING PAPER Money - Part 1, we understand that paper money represents a **form of value** which at the moment cannot be used in trade (because its value is too big) and so as a **substitute** for that **form of value**, paper money was created to be used instead of that **form of value**. Also on the topic of inflation, we know that paper money can lose the value it was originally given. If more paper money is printed into circulation, the value it originally holds decreases. Therefore paper money is not a reliable asset to be kept and held onto.

This time, I would like to address what was briefly touched upon in the last part of inflation concerning paper money. Bluntly, paper money is a medium of exchange, to be used in our country. It was created to serve a purpose. That purpose is to be used by the people to do trade with one another. The ideal destiny of a piece of paper money is to be able to change hands on a daily basis. In other words, if you hold a piece of paper money for more than 3 days, you are being cruel to that piece of paper because by keeping that piece of paper you are not allowing it to fulfill the purpose in its life.

Once again, dear readers, paper money is a medium of exchange. Although it carries purchasing power to give the user the ability to buy things, if you keep any piece of paper money for too long, you are tempting the government to cause inflation which makes every piece of paper money lose its value with regard to the numeric value that appears on that paper.

Sadly, most of us have savings. We store our paper money in our wallets, in our bank accounts, in our private-owned safes, etc. And none of us are willing to part with our money because we are saving it for future use. Some of us don't even know what to use it for. We keep it for the sake of not being poor. Because in our understanding we all agree that those who have little amounts of paper money are the poor and the rich own plenty of paper money. Because we don't want to be seen as poor, we keep the paper money and before we know it, we become hoarders of paper money.

It is a very sad truth that the right way of interacting with paper money is by allowing it to circulate within society. It is a sad truth that by holding on to paper money, we become the bad guys who play a part in ruining the livelihoods of our fellow countrymen. Maybe some of us took notice that there exists amongst us people who do not have savings. Their monthly wage is spent to the last cent every month. But may God be praised because the children of the hoarders of paper money, end up flaunting their parents' money through making large purchases on a daily basis. These children who do this unknowingly help the society that their parents unknowingly tried to harm (by having an unbelievable amount of paper money stored up).

There is a saying that money makes the world go round. And the only way money can do this is if money keeps on circulating amongst us. Although we all hold onto paper money, the ideal way of life, to ensure that the world keeps going round and round, is that we shouldn't be holding on to paper money. The metaphor 'makes the world go round', also implies that the people within the world continue living. So what I am promoting here is that in an open market society, or in a free trade society, paper money that makes the world go round has to be circulated (or transferred from one person to the other) so that life can go on for everyone.

It is indeed the right of any individual to store for themselves their hard-earned wages given to them through the work that they do. But the thing is, paper money is inflatable and prone to a pile of problems if not circulated. In the next **'paper money'** topic which is masked by the title, **'Defining The Fluctuations Of A Country's Currency'**, I would speak more about another reason why paper money is inflatable that has something to do with an open market society (which is an economic system usually found in Democracy and other free trade societies).

The flaw of paper money, which creates the compulsory need to be circulated, is that it was created to represent something and that something has a fixed value. Moving forward, when we reach the part where I disclose the economy of my dream cities conforming to Socialism, you will understand that paper money can have a different destiny — if certain conditions are met, they need not be circulated.

IV. How Investments Aid In The Circulation Of Paper Money

BECAUSE OF THE existence of hoarders (whether intentional or unintentional) of paper money, the circulation of paper money becomes scarce. Therefore as another means to do something about the issue, investments are (from 2015 and surely to this day and beyond) being taught to the citizens and promoted.

For example, a person deposited money to a bank for a period of time, a time deposit investment. At the end of the period of time, the person gets interest. This is what most investments are like. You give your money to be untouched by yourself for a period of time, and whoever you give it to, that party will do something with your money and you end up getting some profit.

What happens normally during government investments where you invest towards the growth of the country is that as a substitute for inflation, the governments seek funding through means of citizen participation of investing in the government projects. In the event of bank investments, what happens is because paper money is needed for formal trade between citizens, and trade amongst citizens cannot be done without paper money, banks give out paper money (as loans) to people who need it in order to do business and during a business, you have to buy goods or services to start the business, therefore money ends up circulating into the economy through the loans that were given. This is how investments work, a means to allow individuals to (unknowingly) partake in the circulation of paper money.

This is why people who have savings, or who withheld paper money, are asked to invest for their future. This is a sales pitch to use your paper money to increase the circulation of paper money in society. Banks may have other motives of profits when they do this but by doing this they also (knowingly or unknowingly) do this good deed to the society.

V. Defining Government Taxation

Supportive Definition References : Their Meanings & Information

---

WHAT IS TAX? Tax is a fee that the government asks the citizens or people living in the country to pay for the well-being of the whole country. It is through the people giving money to the government that allows the government to serve the people with services (eg. police, firefighters, military, etc.) and infrastructures (eg. build or repair roads, transport systems, waterworks, drainage systems, energy sectors, government-owned schools & hospitals, etc.) needed for the operation of both the government and the country itself. Without taxes, any country with a government body, using the open economic system (where the people can directly do trade with other countries), will not be able to function as intended.*

The building of Infrastructure paves the way to giving jobs to workers in the field of construction. When a government provides jobs, what citizens seldom understand is that those jobs are available because of the taxes that we give. In other words, the government plays the part of a financial management system where it finds ways to collect funds and direct the funds collected to finance projects for the social well-being of the whole country.

Taxes do not usually rise for individual people from the middle class downwards. When governments need more money they will increase the taxes of businesses, trade, and wealthy people. This is done in most countries. In some cases, increasing taxes for the people of tomorrow are a means to borrow money from the people of tomorrow to fund today's projects. This is a smart way to prevent inflation.

* (Having finished writing the book and re-reading the last sentence of the first paragraph, I find it to be quite a strange phenomenon don't you think, that without tax, a government body will cease to function, when considering that the government is the **supposed** head of the country. This implies that the supposed head of the country is not the government body but something more sinister, like for example, maybe, paper money itself, making paper money to be the one ruling the country. It sounds like a cult mindset. Because how can we human beings depend on something that is not a living organism. But, this is just my sheer scientific deduction. Because Socialism does not depend on something materialistic in order for society to function, rather it depends on the participation of society, in order to

function. Therefore this mindset from the world of economics presented by the world concerning the use of tax is quite mind-boggling to me, as a Socialist.)

VI. Defining The Fluctuations Of A Country's Currency (Hypothesis)

SUPPORTIVE DEFINITION REFERENCES : THEIR MEANINGS & INFORMATION

I BELIEVE THAT fluctuation of any open country's currency is a product of the currency exchange market's activities that happens when a currency from one country is traded for the currency of other countries. In this topic, we will be opening our minds to the existence of open economies, what they represent and how open economies actually fluctuate the currency of the countries when they each do trade with other countries.

First off, what is an open economy? It is an economic system whereby the individuals and businesses within a country are able to do trade directly with other foreign countries and their peoples. In an open economy, there is a system that helps in this process of trade, that being the currency exchange market. As people buy foreign goods using their credit card or debit card, an exchange between currencies takes place.

There are two economies found to exist with regard to the using of currency. (1) The economy of the country, (2) the economy of the individual, both of which are topics found within the '**Supportive Definition References**' section in this book. The country doing trade amongst other countries in the world stage (where various currencies are present) and the individuals doing trade mostly within their own respective country (where only 1 currency is concerned).

Inflation of the currency and the fluctuation of the currency have the same connotation but I would like to differentiate both of them using the following points. (1) The first one (which I call inflation) is done by allowing more paper money to be printed into society as was talked about in the previous topic of '**Defining Inflation**'. (2) The second one (which I call fluctuation) happens when there is a difference between the value of exports and the value of imports with regards to the paper money currency's numeric value being used in both transactions of the export and import.

The fluctuation of the economy (as per the meaning I gave it), creates the rising and falling of prices when we buy foreign goods. For example, I am from Indonesia using the currency IDR and I want to buy from America. The price of the item that is found in an American shop does not change. If it is $1 today, it should be $1 forever unless changed by the shop owner (probably because of inflation happening in

America). But what changes between today and tomorrow would be the value of my currency (the IDR) against the USD. In other words, how much is $1 today in IDR may be different tomorrow. Today, 1 USD equals 9995 IDR, tomorrow, it may be that 1 USD becomes 9998 IDR. This is called the fluctuation of a country's currency.

Why does this fluctuation happen? It happens because every country has different values in which each of their respective currency is valued at. And because of the different values (just imagine for a moment that society A has 200 tons of gold and prints a total numeric value of 100 thousand $1-bills based on that gold whereas society B has 300 tons of gold and prints a total numeric value of 100 million $1-bills based on that gold) that countries have, when they do trade, because of their inconsistencies in valuing the wealth of their countries (in the example being gold), it will not be fair to make it look like all countries have the same amount of wealth and is using the same method in valuing the wealth of their countries. Therefore the currency exchange market was organized and created as a means of **fairness** and **trust** between countries with regard to the value of their respective currencies, at any current moment, as seen by global markets.

Now how does this currency exchange market work? I do not know how they exactly work but they somehow manage to get the data of exports and imports of countries around the globe that is currently registered as a participant in global markets, they compile the data and then get those varying digits that changes in real-time and show them up on the screen for the world to see.

As can be seen, I have highlighted the words 'fairness' and 'trust'. We should know what fairness implies but what is trust? It is the **confidence placed** unto the value of the currency with regard to another currency. In other words, is the value in currency A really worth this much in currency B. In order for trade to commence between two countries that are using an open economic system in which both countries have their currencies registered in the global market, one has to trust that the other's currency has value. No country wants to do trade with another country that lies about the current value of its currency therefore the currency exchange market takes it into its own hands to validate (through means of tracking inflation, exports, and imports of the countries using the global trade system) the value of currency from any country at any current moment in time.

We have seen the existence of Europe which consists of a group of countries that uses a singular currency. The effect of a single currency to be used amongst countries is to allow for lesser fluctuations of the currency used. Although the currency of Europe which is the Euro, still fluctuates because it does trade with other countries, the Euro remains strong because Europe does trade mainly within its members. The dependency that they have with the outside world is less, due to they having what they already need present amongst themselves. Therefore if a country is heavily dependent on another country, the value of its currency goes down unless there is something that that country could present to the world in such a way other countries are willing to purchase it from them.

The topic on Europe also brings up the theory of a one-world currency and what it may imply to the citizens of the world. I believe what it will do is that it will make the world seem to consists of one big country if everyone uses the same currency where you can do trade with any country using only that same currency. Although this might seem on the surface as a small change in the lives of individuals, but behind the scenes, a one-world currency will prevent the bankruptcy of countries.

Maybe the world witnessed the downfall and default of Greece and deduced that Europe actually failed from an economic standpoint, but in theory, Europe failed because it consists of a body of nations within another body of nations (within the world in other words) meaning that the Euro is a currency amongst the existence of other currencies. The economic theory is that if we have only one currency in existence, used by the world, it would bring about economic stability for all the countries involved because the world as a collective would be able to feed itself and give unto itself the needs and wants of itself, without being dependent on other countries that are using another currency.

But be rest assured, I am not trying to bring the world towards such a direction although the concept of an enclosed economic system is very much similar to the theory of a body of nations feeding itself and providing itself, by itself. But just for a little information, what happens when two countries make a form of union to become one country is that the wealth of both countries are combined together. Just like the example of the islands and gold, if two islands come together, one with 200 tons of gold and another with 300 tons of gold, the total wealth becomes 500 tons of gold, and they print a new single currency based on the existing 500 tons of gold. And so when you imagine the whole world doing this, coming together to form a union of countries, like Europe, we could end up achieving an easier & manageable single currency.

(Although I say that I am not trying to bring the world towards a one-world currency, others who read this book and obtain understanding, may end up being the ones who will try to usher in that one-world currency system.)

VII. Defining An Enclosed Economic Country

"The agenda of any civilization I believe is to be able to be self-sufficient and independent. Socialism also yearns for a self-sufficient and independent society."

TO VISUALIZE AN enclosed economic country is to imagine a pond of water found somewhere in the desert. The waves of the ocean do not reach it. There is no waterway that connects that pond with the ocean. Therefore for the people of the pond to interact with the people in the ocean, it needs some kind of delegators to do it for them. They will not be able to directly interact with the ocean, which is different for those who use an open economic system. Countries using an open economic system are found within the bodies of the ocean where one country could affect the economy of another country.

The advantage of being an enclosed economic country is that it does not participate in the fluctuations of the global economy, in simpler terms, the pond can never do bad things to the ocean and neither can the impacts in any part of the ocean cause any harm to the pond. Because there isn't a participation from the pond to the happenings in the ocean, 1 liter of milk in the pond will be valued as 1 liter of milk in any part of the ocean. But for those within the ocean, the value of 1 liter of milk in one section may not be valued as 1 liter of milk in another section of the ocean.

The disadvantage of being an enclosed economic country is that it has to be self-sufficient in order to prevent the society from falling into a state of anarchy just because of a scarcity in the basic needs of the people. In the event that an enclosed economic country needs something it currently lacks in its society, because it uses a delegator to inquire about its needs, (it) may take a while before its needs can be met. It is because of this one disadvantage of an enclosed economic system, that the world despises governments that use this economic system and call the governments, dictators or tyrants despite their intentions.

The other disadvantage of an enclosed economic system is that because it needs to be self-sufficient, it needs to have either a huge landmass **and** the **varying talents** within the **workforce** to provide for the needs of various living preferences of its citizens, **or** it needs to **force or asks** its citizen **to be okay with** whatever the country can and have the ability to provide for them.

VIII. Defining Universal Basic Income (UBI)

U BI, or also known as Universal Basic Income, is the idea that people, rich or poor, receive a fixed income for all, whether they work or not. This means to say that every month the government will transfer an amount of money to each citizen's bank account even though they do no work at all. And this amount is the same amount for every citizen regardless of anything. Whether the amount given is enough to feed oneself and their partners or families is another issue altogether.

Currently, there are countries that give out free money to their citizens, to the jobless, or to those who are living below the poverty line. UBI is a good thing but it can also bring about a lazy character in people. How does it work? Governments receive money from taxes and from there, distribute some of those taxes to provide UBI for their citizens. Once again the government uses a portion of the hard work done by members of society, to feed society. Quite unfair but as per the wisdom of some governments, this is needed to quell or to prevent society from breaking down.

IX. My Perspective On UBI & The 4th And Future Industrial Revolutions

SUPPORTIVE DEFINITION REFERENCES : THEIR MEANINGS & INFORMATION

A S WAS PREVIOUSLY written, UBI can bring about a lazy character in people. But if the governments do these money handouts equally to all their citizens as to how UBI is supposed to mean, therefore implementing it as we enter into the 4th industrial revolution could be a good way forward.

The next industrial revolution, the 4th industrial revolution, would be the time where technology has come to be given the ability to help mankind in a more direct way. But when we talk about 'industrial', this mostly implies corporations and corporations are businesses and businesses mainly seek profits more than the betterment of society. And so as we enter into a time where technology can finally help reduce our workload, corporations tend to use this opportunity to fill their pockets.

The human workforce is being substituted with a robotic workforce which can do more precise and quick development of goods. The human workforce that usually does services or mental labor will also be substituted by robotic artificial intelligence or software artificial intelligence. When these things happen people will be out of jobs and people who own businesses that have switched to a non-human workforce will inevitably hoard paper money.

Now UBI is a go-to for this future development of civilization if governments play their cards right against corporations.

I would like to open the mind of the individual. America invented the Internet. And during the Obama administration, because the Internet has reached and affected the lives of the world, the UN decided to make the Internet something that can no longer be owned by one country but somehow become control-free in such a way that the people of the world may access it without anyone dictating who can access what.

But whether or not I have just summarized the events of the internet changing hands correctly, what I am trying to emphasize is that if robots (whichever intelligence they have), were to impact the lives of countless of society members, taking jobs away which disallow many to get their hands on paper money, then the best way to tackle the issue is similar to the mindset of the UN. That is to make the robots not be owned by corporations (so that the corporations will not be able to dictate which human being would be able to get their hands on paper money because corporations are the ones who are supposed to distribute paper money as wages to societies) but rather be owned by the government (as being the entity that regulates the workings of society).

It may sound cruel to the corporations or the ones who build robots and gave them intelligence. But I see this way as the only way if people end up losing jobs because of the next industrial revolution.

You may be wondering what exactly do I mean by the government owning the robots (with various intelligence)? Anyone who creates robots or during the event that any robot is created that is used to substitute any form of job that can be done by humans, or was previously done by humans, must be sold to the government supposedly by means of credit (to be paid step by step). The government will not sell the robots to corporations but will charge the usage thereof supposedly to be based on the minimum wage of a human being. Because the government owns these robots, corporations who use robots will have to pay the government that owns these robots and gives paper money in exchange for using these robots in their businesses.

In other words, what can be done is that whichever methods used, the government must own or have a high percentage share in every single robot or artificial intelligence created, and based on the number of human jobs that one robot will do, people who use robots must pay the government a fixed human wage multiplied by the number of human jobs it shall do, or by means of a monthly subscription fee that is not as expensive as a human wage. You are free to do whichever sounds right with regard to the wisdom found in each respective government around the globe. Then with the earnings of the government, it would then execute the bringing about of UBI for its citizens.

Because the 4th industrial revolution, gives technology the means of aiding in the welfare of the people, technology should not be handed over to corporations (businesses that inevitably are seeking profit) but rather to governments (entities that are present in societies whose goal is to manage the harmonious livelihoods of the people).

I just want to add that: if every talent that can be used for society, is used for the goal of a better service towards society, (and not for self-profit), the world will be a better place, not just for regular people throughout the generations but also for the descendants of rich conglomerates and the descendants of inventors and entrepreneurs.

X. Defining Legal Tender

LEGAL TENDER — describes an object that has been officially been announced as something that can be used to exchange for goods or services, in the confines of the country. The paper money found within every country is legal tender inside their own countries. The currency of a country, that has value in the eyes of foreign countries, can be used in those foreign countries in order to do trade with them.

XI. Defining IOU Bills

IOU IS SHORT for 'I Owe You'. This was used in the 1800s by people who had the money or supposedly will soon have the money, but currently in their physical pockets, do not have the money on hand. Either they have the money at home or in the bank or will have the money given to them later, in all these cases those who supposedly have the money will write an IOU bill with the amount owed and give it to the person they owe money to. The person who receives the IOU is supposed to go to the same man that issues the IOU at a later time or place to collect the amount that was written in the IOU bill. After the IOU bill has returned to the writer of the bill, the IOU bill is voided of any exchangeable value.

An IOU bill is voided just like when you use a coupon at a carnival or festival or children's event. Once the coupon has been traded for the items valued at the amount written on the coupon, the storekeeper will punch some holes in the coupon so that the coupons will not be used a second time.

Some people believe that an IOU is actually paper money itself. It isn't, do not be misled. Paper money is created to represent a country's wealth, in the case of the islands we talked about, paper money represents the amount of gold that is in the vaults. Now the gold itself cannot be taken in any amount by anyone as long as there exists paper money that represents it. And so the gold just stays locked up in a vault. This is what it means when paper money is being backed by gold. The wealth exists but it is locked up and cannot be used because it is already being represented in the form of paper money.

(Let me give a further understanding of the gold that is found in the vaults that cannot be touched. That wealth is represented by paper money. People do not trade with gold because it's a hassle therefore paper money was created to represent gold. In other words, the gold that is untouchable in the vaults is what makes paper money to be worth something. The moment the wealth, which paper money represents, vanishes into thin air, foreign countries will no longer see the currency whose wealth had disappeared as having to hold any value anymore which will cause a major fluctuation in currency exchange markets.)

Previously we talked about what paper money is actually, but in the case of the IOU, it is created not because of wealth in existence, but rather to represent an acknowledgment of goodwill that those who hold on to the IOU will get their paper money at a later time. In fact, an IOU can be seen as paper debt. Money has value even after being given back to the bank that issues it. The bank could just hand out the same paper money to other people without having to invalidate it of any value. But a debt needs to be invalidated upon being exchanged for paper money. Therefore a paper debt is a temporary substitute for paper money. And because it is a substitute, it should have the same value.

The reason I added the topic of IOU bills in this book is that I want to be able to allow readers to understand a form of usage that can be done with IOU bills in our modern society.

Let me give a slight example of how paper debt can be a substitute for paper money. Imagine there is a rich person and he has 100 employees working for him in a factory. The wage is $20 per day. Because in the 1800s there isn't a digital transfer monetary system and he currently does not hold $2000, he decides to write each of his employees an IOU of $20. This employer is rich because he owns shops that sell expensive things like furniture and paintings. This man is also respected by the public, everyone knows him. And it is public knowledge that if you want to change the IOU that has his signature on it, you come to his main office and trade the IOU there. Anyone can do this. Now, if there is a table priced at $20 in the furniture shop owned by the rich man, will his signed $20 IOU be accepted there? What does the reader think? I personally believe they may accept it because they could also be paid in IOUs by the same man and at the end of the day go to his main office anyway. What about if the employees use the $20 IOU bill in other establishments not owned by the respected man? Will they be willing to do trade with people paying using IOU bills with his signature on it? They may not but they could because you can trade IOU with paper money in the rich man's main office, or in other words because there is a place they could exchange the IOU bill with paper money, they would accept the IOU bill.

As we know, when the bank prints money, it causes inflation. But is it possible for the banks to print debt? To my understanding, it is possible for the banks to print paper debt with the same numeric amounts paper money is found respectively (eg. $1, $2, $5, $10, $20, $50, etc.) without causing inflation, **if and only if**, the laws surrounding the use and distribution of paper debt, is followed to the letter. As long as every paper debt is treated as paper debt, banks should be able to print paper debt without causing inflation.

What is the use of printing paper debt? The use is this. Because governments need money to pay for its programs that will be done by local citizens or foreign citizens living in the country, also needing money to pay its military, police, and other government departments and personnel, governments could print paper debt and give payments using paper debt, because one way or another paper money is going to land in the hands of governments by means of taxes. It is because paper money is going to return to the government, the government should be able to print paper debt up to 50% of the current amount of paper money in existence.

What governments may need to do and consider when printing paper debt is that there is an expiration date on the paper debt. When a paper debt has passed that expiration date, the government, having received paper debt may have to wait a period of time before reprinting that paper debt. The paper debt also has a limited amount that can be printed. There must be a limit that does not surpass 100% of the paper money in existence. Why? Because when you do trade with other countries, you will need to do trade using paper money and not using paper debt. Therefore when a person goes on a holiday outside the country, he will need to bring paper money and not paper debt. Paper debt can only be used within the confines of the country it was issued in and cannot be traded for other currencies in money changers. Citizens also must be given the right to exchange their paper debt with paper money when they need it for trade with other countries. If you print paper debt more than a certain percentage of paper money in existence, when the people want to do trade with other countries, there may be a lack of paper money in existence to trade with paper debt.

For paper debt to work within society, the government has to issue it as a form of **legal tender** that can be used only in the country. And because society knows that it is paper debt and not paper money they may choose not to receive paper debt from anyone, therefore the government may need to give some extended value to paper debt (eg. there will be discounts when you use paper debt to purchase, this or that, goods or services, from government-owned establishments or businesses that work with governments, or something like that). But every paper debt will most likely have the same value as paper money because it is a temporary substitute for paper money, **and it is only to be used within the confines of the country**.

This is just a hypothesis of how an IOU can be seen to be and be used to lessen the burdens of government. If there is a way to print value without causing inflation, this would be one of the ways to do it but because the world consists of multiple currencies, people will always need paper money to do trade with other countries.

XII. Defining Government Bonds

WHAT ARE GOVERNMENT bonds? Government bonds are actually a type of IOU. In the case of the IOUs used in the 1800s, which were mostly used by corporations to pay their employees at a later time, where at that point in time when the IOU was issued, it was issued and given to the employee as a note of debt **in exchange for the services of the employee on that particular day**, which then, will be paid at a later time. But with government bonds, the issuing of the said government bonds is given in exchange not for services, but rather in exchange for paper money. This is usually done because the government currently is in need of the paper money for some reasons. And the specialty of a government bond is that it grants some profit (an interest based on the agreement with the government previously) to the investor when he / she comes to collect their money from the government at a later time.

This being said, I would like the readers to know that there is a difference between what I said about 'printing paper debt' previously with the widely known 'government bonds'. With the knowledge of the IOU that brings about the term that I call 'paper debt', 'paper debt' does not necessarily require the governments or banks that changes 'paper debt' for 'paper money' to give the 'paper money' with additional interests when being exchanged for 'paper debt' that has the same nominal amount. In other words, when 'paper debt' valued at $10 is exchanged, it would get 'paper money' valued at $10 as well. (The only exception being the usage of 'paper debt', as a means to get discounts when purchasing from businesses and services that are partnering with the government.)

XIII. Defining Barter

WHAT IS BARTER? The informal definition is trading something in exchange for something else. You trade milk for bread. You trade a cow for sheep. In our modern societies, we use paper money to buy milk or bread. But a long time ago, people trade directly. When a person needs something, they check their inventory and bring items from it and go to their neighbors and say, "These are the items that I have, what can I give you in such a way that you are willing to give me what I need." And from there they do an agreement and directly trade things for other things. In conclusion, barter is giving something to someone as a means of wanting something else in return for it. As for the formal definition, barter is the form of doing trade with others without using money.

(This understanding of barter will be needed when we talk about trade between countries that do not affect the economy of any parties involved.)

XIV. Defining The Economy Of The Country

WHAT IS THE economy of the country? It is the financial management of the country. It is the value of wealth, the value of the country's currency. One of the means of calculating this is through exports and imports, all the spendings of people within the country with regard to foreign goods or services and also the spending of foreign people from other countries with regard to the goods and services within the country. In other words, the money that goes out from the country and the money that comes into the country defines the current economy of the country. Another term used to describe the economy of the country is GDP.

As was previously touched upon, in **'Defining The Fluctuations Of A Country's Currency'** found in the **'Supportive Definition References'** section in this book, the fluctuations of a country's currency being valued at a current value as seen by other currencies, depend on this GDP. A country with a good GDP score is a country with more money coming into it than compared to money going out from it. Because a **currency** can be **bought** or **sold** in exchange for other currencies. Therefore in terms of currency, a country with a good GDP score is one whose currency is bought by foreign people more than it is sold.

When a country's GDP is high, the business world tends to see it as being something good. A high GDP represents a growing country. Because a country's wealth (gold in vaults) is limited and is being represented by paper money (a country's currency), if a country's GDP (value in their currency as seen by other countries) increases, therefore there will always be another country out there that is within the confines of the ocean of global economies, that is currently having its currency valued lower than when it was in the beginning when trade first commenced.

A country that is starting to grow or has famine within the country, will surely need to buy food outside their country. As they buy food from the outside, their currency value decreases as seen through the eyes of foreigners because they are using their paper money to buy another country's paper money which increases that other county's currency whereas weakening its own currency. Trade amongst countries is like a balance sheet in accounting, at the end of the day because the wealth (gold in vaults) of both countries remain the same, the value of paper money changes to suit the GDP; one country will always be lower than the other.

When I see this GDP which everyone loves to talk about, what I see is a push from the world to have more exports than imports. It comes down to competition. It comes down to business. It comes down to profit. There is something sinister going on here. It is as though Capitalists are behind the creation of the word 'GDP' and promoting it as a term that defines a country's growth, and that every country's economy can grow at the same time. What does the reader think?

Paper money in any country represents the wealth (that can never increase but is fixed) of that country. The term currency means : paper money belonging to a country. We have something fixed being represented by inflatable paper money. We have to use currency to purchase other currencies when doing trade with other countries. If this is the case, can **every** country at any second in time have its exports more than its imports?

I believe it can't be done. Because it cannot be done, GDP cannot mean growth because growth doesn't do damage to someone else. Every tree can grow taller together. Every human being can have growth in skills and knowledge together. But the economies (supposedly based on currencies that are based on paper money, that is again based on fixed wealth) of countries cannot grow together because they are restrained by something limited. Because of this when the value of a country's currency rises, another country's currency actually has to fall to accommodate that rise. And the media usually portrays the fall of a country's currency because of a lack of management from the part of the government or sitting president and is depicted as a bad thing and gives a bad name to that president, when actually it isn't wrong to choose not to harm someone else.

XV. Defining The Economy Of The Individual

SUPPORTIVE DEFINITION REFERENCES : THEIR MEANINGS & INFORMATION

JUST AS IT is with the economy of the country, the economy of the individual is the going out and coming in of paper money for an individual. It is his spendings against the money he receives.

As we all know, paper money is a part of everyone's life. Should a man forfeit his life or should we allow him to forfeit his life just because he has no paper money to buy food? It is for the sake of being human that we say no. But who do you think, which type of people will say yes to the question presented? What kind of (moral and ethical) values does the person who will answer 'yes', have?

Paper money is viewed as something of value. And because it represents wealth that is fixed in amount, the more paper money a person has, the more power he may be seen to have. It is difficult to change a person's mindset towards paper money. The only fault that brings about this mindset in people is that paper money is printed as a representation of something limited in amount.

[Imagine if paper money is printed as a representation of the livelihood of society. In this imagination, what becomes the representation of paper money, what is the amount present, and what is the limit? Every life in society continues as long as society exists. Therefore what is paper money printed out from? Can paper money be printed based on coexistence? As long as my neighbor who is a carpenter exists, I can get wooden furniture. As long as farmers exist, I get food. As long as engineers exist, things can be fixed. The conclusion is that as long as we all play a part in society, we live and continue living. And based on our livelihoods, paper money is printed to represent it. This paragraph speaks about the imaginative minds of early Socialists.]

The economy of the individual mostly depends on employers. If any value is seen by the employer to be within the individual, the employer employs the individual to become an employee and give wages to the individual in exchange for work. It is the employer's job to distribute paper money to his employees.

But the economy of the employer depends on the profits of his business and in order for him to have profits, people must be willing to buy his goods or services.

It is because of the two previous paragraphs that the economy of any individual is dependent upon the trading done within society. Both individuals and those who are employers must continue going about their lives in the purchase of goods & services, all the while having an income stream to accommodate their purchases. This once again brings the need for the circulation of paper money, to and fro, from one person to the next and so on, on a daily basis.

In the case of the economy of the individual, as should be also the case for the economy of the country, the economy is only healthy and ideal if the money coming in does not stay in for a long time but also has to go out, if possible equally in amount as the money coming in. By doing it this way the hoarders of paper money will not restraint the fluent flow of paper money in circulation but let it flow out as how it comes in. It is likened to breathing, where the amount of air that comes into the body will eventually come out and will be replaced by the same amount. This is how a body continues to live. Therefore, for a society to live, the same should be done. This is the philosophy of it.

XVI. Another IOU Example To Help Envision A Society That Uses IOU

IMAGINE THERE IS a billionaire who owns an orphanage consisting of 200 children. This billionaire owns a public school, a public swimming pool, a public zoo, public hair salon, a public food court, and others. This billionaire lives in America with these 200 children who are housed in an orphanage for free. But these public places that the billionaire has, are not there for free. These public businesses, which are situated near one another, sell to the public and also to these 200 children.

In America, the currency is in US dollars. And every week this billionaire gives pocket money to every child of the orphanage. But because he does not want any of the children to misuse their pocket money, he gives them an IOU instead, in their respective bills: 5 cents, 10 cents, 20 cents, 50 cents, 1 dollar, 2 dollars, 5 dollars, 10 dollars. The total amount each child gets is $200 in IOU bills. These public stores that the billionaire owns are given IOU bills to give returns to children who purchase their goods or services with IOU bills. This is done so that children who pay with IOU bills get also in return IOU bills and not US dollars which could be misused to buy drugs and such. But when $200 are not enough, what any of the children could do is sell something that they themselves make to their fellow brothers and sisters, and in exchange for what they sell, they would be able to receive more IOUs to add to their $200 worth of IOUs a week.

At the end of the day, these public stores, trade with the billionaire the excess IOU bills that are in their stores, in which they begot from the orphaned children, with US dollars, and also renew the IOU bills that they have so that they might have enough of each bill to give returns to the orphaned children on the next day. (The reason these people working in these public places need to trade the excess IOU bills with US dollars is because these people have a life outside the system of the billionaire.)

After several years, more orphaned children are admitted to the orphanage owned by this billionaire, and also more public businesses are created into existence. Some of the original 200 children went away but most of them remained. Some from these most-that-remained decided to work in the public businesses owned by the billionaire but they choose to also have a life outside the system of the billionaire. Whereas the others, **choose to both live and work** within the system of the billionaire.

Now, I would like to highlight the lives of those who choose to both live and work within the system of the billionaire. These young adults receive payments in both IOUs and US dollars and no longer do they need to trade the IOU, which they received, with US dollars, because they live within the system and do not need anything outside of the system. When they want to buy from any store within the system, they can use both the US dollars along with the IOU in any transaction because the public businesses in the system receive both as payment.

Let the people who read this book think and understand the possibility of implementing this IOU system in your countries.

These are the characteristics of the IOUs found in the story :

(1) No matter how many of these IOUs are printed, no harm is done towards the US dollar / economy

(2) When the people who live and work in the system, wants to go out, then only they need US dollars

(3) The US dollar is a global currency, but the IOU acts as a local currency — used only in the system

According to a friend, the billionaire can only allow the printing of IOUs with regard to how much he has in his bank account. Meaning that the IOUs made under the name of the billionaire that are currently in circulation cannot be more than the money he has locked up in his bank (within the duration in which the IOUs are in circulation). But according to my understanding, as long as IOUs can be used to live within the system, there is no need to exchange IOUs with US dollars unless the person wants to go out of the system for holiday, in which case US dollars (a global currency) is needed.

[Note 1 : Every country's currency, as long as the country has opened its borders to trade amongst one another directly without the use of barter, is a global currency.]

[Note 2 : A country that cannot trade directly, uses barter because that country is a pond in the desert away from the ocean. Whereas a country that does trade directly with one another is a body of water inside the ocean and is prone to suffer the effects from any troubled bodies of water.]

Note 2 has nothing to do with the current topic at hand but I just want to bring it up for it has connections with

Note 1 and also has connections with the implementation of an enclosed economic system used within my planned Socialistic cities. The reason I am capable of coming up with this IOU system is because of the similarities in which are found in the economy that I had planned for the Socialistic cities.

Returning to the topic at hand. I have in the story above a billionaire. Now let's **substitute** the billionaire with a country. Every business in the country is in the confines of the country — is a part of the country's so-called 'system'. The citizens of the country both live and work inside the country. They require nothing outside the country. In the story above, there are 3 groups of people who parallel those who exist in our physical world. (1) The people who work and live outside the system but at times purchase goods and services from within the system. (2) The people who only work inside the system but need to interact outside the system to get ingredients and other materials that are not found within the system. (3) The people who do both '(2)' which is work, and at the same time live in the system. The people who are categorized as group 1, are foreigners. The people who are categorized as group 2, are businessmen who own companies, who also need to restock supply from foreign lands. Lastly, the people who are categorized as group 3, are people who work as employees and purchase goods / services from the businesses within the confines of the country. Group 2 and 3, aside from purchasing foreign goods to restock their wares, only need the global currency when they want to go overseas on trips or holidays.

This is the idea of the IOU system that I would like to present to all countries, in hopes that your citizens may live far better lives rather than living a life where the currency is inflated every year which causes the savings of hard-working people who are not educated in investments or are afraid of investments, to lose the value of their hard-earned savings. This IOU system, if capable of being implemented, will put aside the need to inflate the currency of your country. Because whenever the government needs to pay people living in the country, they can do so by printing IOUs as wages or payment which acts as a local currency of the country and will be received by any business in the confines of the country. When people are in need of the global currency, they are capable of going to banks to trade their local currency with a global currency. The moment the IOUs are returned to the government, the IOUs are invalidated. (Why would anyone want to hold IOUs? Because when they pay taxes or use government places, they get a 20% discount when paying with IOUs. Something like this will attract the people to holding onto IOUs while living inside the country. And they will only hold your country's global currency when they want to go out for holidays or to restock their supply of goods or to get materials / ingredients not found in the country.) If the government is in need of the global currency to do trade with other countries, the government will then ask its citizens who have the global currency and trade those with newly printed IOUs.

People who ask the question why inflation does not happen when we print IOUs, this is because there is a difference between a global currency and a local-confined currency. Printing a local-confined currency does not affect the global currency. As long as it is differentiated, and remains differentiated, inflation does not happen. As long as that local-confined currency is not accepted by money exchangers to be used to buy other currencies and is not accepted by other countries as an extended global currency from that country, inflation will not happen. For the moment that local-confined currency is seen as a global currency, inflation will happen. But similar to the story above, where the billionaire owns the public businesses, no matter how many IOUs he created, as long as all the businesses remain inside his system and the businesses receive IOU bills as payment, people live normally, and the US dollar is unaffected.

[What most socialist fail to see and understand is that in order to print money without inflation happening is to first own every farmland, every supply of animal for food, every business in such a way that people can rely on the country for all its needs. This creates a country that is self-sufficient and self-dependent. Therefore the government only needs to trade with other countries not for its needs but rather for what it wants or for secondary needs. And then you implement a local-confined currency for the people to use inside the confines of the country and with this currency, you can print without restraint. As long as the people understand and care for one another, this system will not be misused and although the country may not increase in technological advancements, this country will certainly not die out of hunger for it has everything it needs inside it that sustains life and the living of its citizens. The downside of this country is that during a famine where disease strikes the animals and trees and vegetation, the country will end up having to do trade with other countries for survival. This is the only downside of an economy-secluded country. (But this is not what my Socialist cities will be; Trade amongst those outside will also still be present but not in the way it is modernly done.)

Socialists who believe they can print money without inflation are not deluded. You can do so but with certain aspects needed to be placed in mind. The environment must meet a certain list of criteria before you are allowed to print local-confined currency (but not global currency) without restraint.]

SECOND GRAND CHAPTER : DEMOCRACY & ITS ALLOWED EVILS OF THE WORLD RESULTING IN HARDSHIPS

Preferring Socialism Over Democracy : Envisioning Cities Of Societal Harmony & Continual Coexistence

I. Defining Democracy

FIRST OF ALL, what is Democracy according to people? If we ask people directly what will their responses be?

Democracy is (1) a system of government where the people are represented by elected officials who are elected through a system of voting held by the whole population, elected by means of a majority outcome. In other words, a participation of the whole population being given the right to elect based on their own will, a government of their choosing, where those who end up choosing the party or person not holding a majority of the votes, will have to deal with it because it is what makes the **majority** of the population **happy**. (In Democracy, one cannot please everyone because the values of people are different and are **allowed** to be different.)

Democracy is (2) the right of every individual to be given the freedom of thought, freedom of religion, freedom of values, freedom of political opinion, freedom of perspectives, and freedom of consciences. (In Democracy, people are given the right to be different from others and to have a different mindset than others. Democracy allows the voicing out of various forms of justice that a person may feel right to be done unto himself which may be wrong in the understanding of others. In other words, it allows people to use logical sense to justify that they are right when others believe they are wrong.)

Democracy is (3) the freedom to do trade directly from one person in one country to another person in another country. (Democracy allows any people within the country to sabotage their own countries' wealth and their countries' economic ranking that will cause others within the country to feel the impact thereof because of the actions of making too many imports. I would like to also highlight that when individuals buy from abroad, their spendings also affect the economy of the country. This brings out the fact that it is business corporations and open markets that causes the fluctuation of our economies. Because of this knowledge, the free market actually allows any mastermind to make use of this flaw to make other countries poorer with time whilst strengthening his own country's currency.)

Democracy is (4) the freedom to own your own business. (Democracy allows people to own a business. And business allows people to get richer, to hoard and keep more amounts of paper money than they spend on a daily basis. This gives them the ability to sabotage the livelihoods of their fellow countrymen by hoarding paper money and forcing governments to inflate the currency. Foreign companies are also allowed to enter and take the profits made within the country back to their home country, deteriorating the value of a country's currency.)

There could be more than these 4 points but Democracy gives individuals the right to various kinds of Freedom which brings about the existence and availability towards these four points and many others. (eg. to have rights, to own land or property, to be protected by rights or laws, etc.)

II. Societal Problems Within Democracy

THE SOCIETY IN a democracy consists of people with various problems that **happen to come upon** them because of a great deal of freedom that is found and allowed to exist within Democracy. And it is because of these problems that these people face which are not being treated or which are not being healed, that causes the existence of every other problem in society which damages the whole society and creates morally bad people and all forms of evil. One example is this. Because a man is treated badly by members of society, he is prone to the probability that he himself will end up treating someone else badly. There is a ripple effect or a chain reaction that eventually goes through the whole society.

There is a saying that goes like this, "Money is the root of all evil." Yes, profit-seeking people will trample on others in order for them to get those profits. But there is also an understanding that says, "Unrestrictive freedom allows the intentions of evil people to flourish." Unsupervised freedom will eventually give rise to a form of curiosity followed by a motivation to inflict evil.

Every person has 2 choices that they struggle with, on a daily basis. Either I do this bad thing or I do that good thing. What then will be the outcome when no one is looking? How many percent of the men in the world will try to manipulate a very attractive but currently hypnotized girl knowing that no one is looking or recording, and how many will abstain from doing anything at all? Evil is tempting. If hypnotism is real and I have the chance to say to that girl, "The moment you snap out of that hypnotized state, you will find yourself in love with me," will I not say it? She could be married or is engaged to a loving man, yet I ruin her future or life by doing a form of sabotage. It may seem harmless to change her perspectives for my self-interest, but this is known as an act of evil moral conduct in society (which may have begun through mischief or playful innocence but once the pride or the good sensation has reached the heart, men will continue doing it just to feel good about themselves and bring about a deterioration of moral conduct in that person which will eventually contaminate the behaviors of his surrounding people).

The seed of evil exists in the hearts of every individual from birth. There is no way to rid the heart of evil. Whether we allow for evil to grow within our hearts depends on the individual. It is not that we shouldn't trust individuals to make the right choices but because there exists the probability of anyone for that matter to do evil, Socialism tends to restrict everyone in society. This is why I say Socialism is wise and gentle. Socialism understands the inevitable behaviors of the society, therefore we counter using restrictions.

Moral issues, good values, holy living, choosing right from wrong. These factors are outside the reigns of Democracy. The ideas and ideals that form the values of Democracy do not demand a particular value or character trait from anyone. In fact, it does the opposite — it allows and defends anyone who has a different value. (This is prone to be exploitable.)

No one can know the heart of any person. It is not possible to catch a bad person before he does a bad thing, because there is always a possibility, no matter how small it is, that at the last moment he may choose not to put into actions, his bad intentions. But this does not mean that freedom should be given while we all allow nature, instincts, and chemical reactions to shape society. Again this does not mean that freedom should be given whilst we all close our eyes and hope for the best because the best will never come as long as there are (1) people who have bad values or evil intent or the willingness to screw someone over, or the want to be better than others, and (2) chances or open opportunities that tempts people to be wicked or tempts them to chase after self-interests.

Freedom tempts every human being and every human being struggles to choose between right and wrong. The paring up of Democracy with human beings (who originally was created to act on instinct and natural impulses **unless** they received intelligence through good parenting, religion, or philosophy) is a gamble which scientifically speaking will likely lean more towards the fulfilling of human-desired ego-centric self-interests. This union will result in disasters because all we need is a handful of people with self-interest and the whole country may end up living in poverty because those 10 people, for example, hoard 35% of the total country's wealth in the form of paper money. Democracy should not be paired up with people who basically can do evil because those who can, **will do evil**. Only those who have **a strong reason** not to choose evil will not do evil. (Therefore Socialism does not persecute religion because good religion helps in the building up of members in society — giving them that strong reason.) Sadly the people in this world have not reached the consciousness of coexistence and so as intellectuals, we have to suppress freedom in order to fill up the requirements for harmony.

III. Democracy, According To America

SECOND GRAND CHAPTER : DEMOCRACY &
ITS ALLOWED EVILS OF THE WORLD
RESULTING IN HARDSHIPS

PEOPLE HAVE ALWAYS believed that Democracy is the true and fair ideology to be used. America is a nation built on Democracy. And because America believes Democracy to be a good ideology, it imposes Democracy to be used and implemented in nations across the globe. Those who resist this **'form of goodwill'** from America are sanctioned and given a form of punishing treatment.

(What a person deems good, he will try and ensure that other people conform to that same goodness. This is what I previously talked about in previous topics. The characteristics of a good intellectual person are like this. He tries to make other people conform to what he believes is good. Every leader or person with a set of ideals will always think that whatever he believes in, that is to be done to the people, is for the greater good, according to his own mind, which may not necessarily be seen as something 'good' by the people who are affected by it.)

America sees Democracy as that good ideology that the world must also follow. And the world sees America as the father of Democracy. Americans themselves believe that their country of America conforms to 100% democratic values. But what Americans forget is that America is not just built on Democracy but also under the effect of the religious belief of their founding fathers, which is Christianity. The founding fathers of America founded America and apply their Christian beliefs to the constitution of America. What I am trying to say is that, what the people in America know to be as Democracy, is actually Christian Democracy — a democracy based on Christian values or a democracy that has religious values (**already existing beforehand**) in its society.

Therefore, when America proposes other nations to conform to Democracy, America is actually asking other nations to conform to a Democracy whereby the people beforehand are supposed to have values conforming to Christian values. So there is a big misunderstanding unbeknownst by both parties (by America and the other country it is imposing on) towards the meaning of America. America does not actually know that what they believe to be a Democracy is actually a Democracy whereby the people themselves have conformed to Christian values. Whereas the countries that they propose Democracy to, see what America means, as Democracy to be 100% pure Democracy (without having the need for Christian values to be a part of society first). Because of this, those who decided to follow America to becoming democratic end up with a different Democracy than the Democracy that America sees itself to have (which is the Democracy whereby the people conform to good values). The Democracy of the other countries that are affected by America to be Democratic, ends up with a Democracy that may not be the same as how they see America itself to have. (The Democracy that does not have people conforming to good values within society becomes a Democracy that is filled with injustice and unfair practices.)

America believes that Democracy is a good thing because the people in America consist of religiously good human beings and so evil was almost non-existent in their society in the early beginnings of America because the people were already conforming to religious values. That was in the past. Today the citizens in America no longer retain those good values of Christianity and have become secular. But Americans still believe that Democracy is good because of their past **experience** and knowledge about how America was during previous generations, and they currently do not blame Democracy for its current secular state, instead, they blame it on the diminishing moral conduct of individuals in society that no longer conforms to Christian values, that came to be either because of the entry of unbelieving immigrants into America or the impact of foreign influence and mindset on the children of America.

America is founded through Christian values. And there is a huge difference between religious democracy and 'democracy' period (full stop). From an early Socialist standpoint, our restrictions and regulations in Socialist societies prevent evil hearts from becoming actions, in other words, the enemy of Socialism are those with evil intent towards their fellow citizen. From my personal understanding, Democracy can only be better than Socialism **if and only if** the people (I mean every single person, without exceptions) living in the confines of the Democratic societies are **religiously good people** that **do not have evil intent** towards their fellow neighbor.

If we have a society where every single individual is religiously good or conforms to a moral conduct of goodness, then the society does not need to fear of thefts, scams, murder, abortion, scandal, adultery, slavery, fornication, unfair wages, mistreatment of fellow members of society, and so on. They do not have to fear towards these behaviors because everyone in society is religiously good. But this can never be achieved with Democracy unless the people (everyone in society) themselves have a **willingness** and a moral conscience **to restrict themselves** from doing any evil thing to their neighbor.

(This is why Socialism enters into the lives of the people in order to do what the ideologies of the world could not do. This is why early Socialists build **new** communities where the people willingly want the same thing.)

Democracy is a set of ideas and ideals that allows people to have freedoms in their life. This is a freedom to do whatever they can do to be or feel happy. Once again America's Democracy is understood as Democracy conforming to Christian values. And when you put Christian values over a democratic country, what you are doing is telling people, "Hey, this is what we should do." But you are simply telling them and not dictating them.

Having a conscience is the same as having a choice. A conscience to do good or to do bad comes back to the wants of the person. Whether I want to conform to that value, under democracy, is my choice. The bottom line is that by putting Christian values together with Democracy, you are just asking the people to conform to good values of the Christian religion but because Democracy is the personal freedom to do what makes a person happy, that person may choose to go against the Christian values and Democracy will not be able to condemn that person because it is a Democracy — a freedom for the individual personal life and preferences, which include his values, views, and beliefs.

I know that a democratic society is under law but the Christian values themselves are not all within the law. Also because values are what makes people different it will not be possible to put every Christian value into law under Democracy. Because Democracy does not allow you to force people to conform to a certain value. Religious values are good to have in society but they can only be achieved by the willingness of the society. (I say the following to Christians : "That is why the Christian deity according to the scriptures will rule the earth with a rod of iron." In other words, rule with a forced arm. This way the Holy God will enforce His character, which is Holiness, unto the people and ensure that the people live lives that reflect His being and at the same time obey the laws placed, throughout the 1000 years, else direct punishment will come upon them.) Once again, values cannot be put as laws because it tends to change the personality or the character of the person and this form of changing a person's values under a democratic constitution is not allowed by the mindset of Democracy. When you try to change a person's value, you will end up being forceful to that person with regard to his personal freedom whereas being forceful is not a Democratic trademark.

You cannot merge Democracy with Christian values and hope the people be good people. It is the people (everyone in society) themselves that must have a good moral conscience that will allow a Democratic society to consist of good people.

The reason I put 'everyone in society' in parenthesis whenever I have the word 'people' is because if it is everyone minus 1 person, that one person can bring about the downfall of the rest of society. Therefore it is a compulsory that everyone must be good inside a democratic society for that democratic society to be better than that of a restricted socialist society.

(Additional info, Socialists do not force a value unto the people. We do hope that the people have good moral values. We do hope that the people understand our reasoning for our intrusive laws and regulations. But in order to ensure harmony, we choose the path of restricting the movements and actions of all the people to quell any problem in society.)

And so when American pastors say that Socialism is bad and Democracy is good because they previously lived in an environment where the people conforms to a religious understanding of moral conduct, the Democracy that they call good is under a **biased** interpretation of it, whereby Democracy is put upon a religious society. Because a religious society consists of people not choosing to do evil or restricts themselves to doing evil, therefore Democracy in America (or any society conforming to good values) looks like a good thing — it looks like justice and fairness. Whereas **pure** Democracy itself, without a society that willingly conforms to good values (like America in its early days), will be filled with evil people and have future complicated problems in society.

All these being said, I want the reader to understand that the Democracy of America is a different Democracy than that of pure Democracy. The Democracy of America **as believed by the Americans themselves**, (let me say once more) is a Democracy whereby the people are understood to have conformed themselves to good religious values and good moral actions / behaviors. Whereas Democracy **itself** is a set of ideas and ideals that no matter the values of any person existing in society, allows personal freedom of preferences / values, regardless of what their neighbor's values are.

In the following topic of this Grand chapter concerning Democracy, I will bring about the hidden faces of Democracy which I deemed as uncivilized practices found within Democracy itself because of the massive freedom allowed to exist within democratic societies.

IV. The Hidden Faces Of Democratic Freedom

JUST AS A side note before this big chapter begins : everything written here is trying to give an understanding to the reader concerning the evils that may appear or have appeared in society because society was given democratic freedom. There could be some confusing topics but the motive is to bring light to the atrocities that a fellow citizen is willing to do towards his fellow citizen because of the evil within his heart to be better than others, etc. So this big chapter elaborates on the various evils that are being done either legally (which are acceptable to the law because the person who did evil does evil whilst obeying the law) or secretly (trying their best to not get caught) within society.

The government will not be able to do anything in a country where democratic freedom is present. There are all sorts of freedom and anyone can get away with anything. As long as contracts are signed, as long as laws are made under freedom, although injustice abounds, the President, no matter how good-natured the man is, can do little to help his fellow citizens who are facing hardships at a personal level which were caused by their fellow citizens in society.

In a country where rich groups of people are hoarding paper money whilst the people are suffering, all the President can do is to tell them not to hoard paper money. He cannot arrest them for hoarding paper money, not because he is not capable of doing so, but rather because the democratic law disallows it, and the President is under the law. That is why many of the rich hate Socialism because they rather live outside of Socialism where they can attain power in their riches. That is why the elite uses democracy as bait for the masses and the masses take the bait because of the word 'Freedom' which is a setup. You get freedom but you lose justice.

The people must understand that freedom does not mean justice. In fact, freedom allows for injustice. Freedom allows for all sorts of things like beliefs, values, perspectives, etc. This is what Freedom allows : it allows both the good and the bad to change the world — to do unto the world whatever they believe benefits or is meaningful / useful to them. With freedom given, on one hand, the good want to bring light to what is just. But with that same freedom, the bad wants to stay hidden while continuing in what they want to do without being caught and so the bad, at the end of the day find all sorts of ways to divert attention, uses subtle wordings, to commit acts of evil whilst hiding behind laws, hiding behind terms & conditions, hiding behind democracy.

Freedom gives the right for anyone to dictate (either openly or subtly) how anyone should live their lives. It is because of this that I would like the readers to open their minds to all the various hidden faces of Democratic Freedom, even those that are not written in this book. Anything can happen when you give the world Freedom. And because Freedom equals Rights, therefore even bad people end up with Rights and no Democratic government or Democratic ideology can do anything about this problem because as long as the evil people in Democracy are clever enough, they will be able to use Democracy itself as a shield to protect themselves.

"Religion is intolerant to whatever makes God angry or displeases God but Democracy is tolerant to just about anything."

In Democracy, laws are made and there are ones that are made that can be twisted and misused to protect those who are evil at heart. And then they make Socialism sound offensive to the masses because of the fact that Freedom certainly cannot exist within Socialism, full stop, not continuing on to say that because a probability exists where freedom that is given to all may end up being used by unstoppable people, even unstoppable by the President, to commit injustice to the people. And they brand this 'injustice' as life itself — as the norms of living.

(I personally do not agree that the injustice that every person may end up facing should be seen as one of the norms of living in society. People like to declare that the hardships that you face as you live, is life. "That's life," they say. I believe that life can be made easy and because it can be made easy, it should be made easy for all our sakes. If a man can prevent hardships from being faced by his fellow countryman because of what he himself does, he should. For all our sakes, everyone who can, should. This is my take.)

The people surely want freedom because it is supposed to be good. Yes, it will be good where evil does not exist. But where evil exists and freedom also is allowed for them, the people will suffer. And no President can say that freedom will only be given to this group of people but not that group of people. Because we don't know who is evil at heart.

"Every man is born precious to God. No man should come and scam another. Every man is born pure at heart. If wickedness is found in one man's heart and he causes another to become as wicked as him, will anyone with a good conscience allow this? Over my dead body. I will shut him up before he could cause the pure at heart to turn evil. This is the Socialism I intend to bring about."

1. Employers, Employees, Jobs & The Workplace

I BETTER STATE the summary up here : what will be found in this particular sub-chapter is this — that jobs play a huge part in the stability of society in terms of giving financial aid to the employees who are individuals in our society. It is because of jobs that individuals get the income to buy their daily food. All of us who have worked before can deduce many scenarios where this whole sub-chapter may lead to, concerning the conscious (or unconscious) mistreatments towards employees, indirectly (or directly) being done by companies. Socialism is against giving power to businesses or individuals to have employees, or to even exist because many evils can be done by a business or by individuals if power is allowed for them to ensure the flow of money from one person to the next. This sub-chapter hopes to bring insights as to how work and jobs should be a government problem instead of allowing corporations to be the distributors of paper money.

What is the workplace? It is the place where people work.

What is a job? It is a position (eg. carpenter, engineer, manager, etc.) that exists in the workplace where the person does a particular form of work that describes his position.

What is an employee? Anyone that is employed to do a job (or service), in exchange for wages (or salary).

What is an employer? A person or organization that gives work to someone and pays them for the job done.

It is from the job that employees do in a workplace, that they end up receiving money (from their employer) in order to live and **continue living**. Anything that happens in the workplace, because the workplace provides for the continual living of any individual, will have an effect on the individual itself. An accumulation of bad experiences (surrounding work) may change the individual and cause bad values to appear within his being.

Because the employer is the one who gives the wages, power is in the hands of the employer towards the employee. This gives the connotation that the employer is above the employee, although both are in fact fellow human beings.

And whenever we speak about power, it can be misused. (It all comes back to the conscience and moral values of the one in power.)

In most cases, it is the employee that is the victim of the working world led by private ownerships of corporations and businesses. Bluntly speaking, what are the mishaps of an employee? (1) Unemployment — due to employers being choosy or the lack of experience from the person itself, or even because of competition between employers, unemployment may befall members of society. (2) Unfair wages — there exists a certain trend in society where employees with much working experience are given wages at a rounded-up value of the government minimum wage (in some cases — not rounded up at all); although these employees are waged far below their value worth in experiences, the law does not condemn the employer because the employees are waged above the minimum wage. And the employers themselves are happy because they see themselves as law-abiding citizens. There are also instances of unfair wages that the reader may see found in factories or other jobs in existence that although are useful to society as a whole but are given low wages for their services to society (eg. garbage collectors, sewage cleaners, and other unwanted positions in society). (3) Mistreatment towards current position — an employee who has a position in the company is asked to do other things unrelated to his position without any form of incentives. (4) Laying Off Of Employees — due to a decline in company profits, the company may have to lay off their employees or declare bankruptcy and disband the whole company.

These are the four things that could happen to an employee that is hired by an employer whose goal is profit. Because of these, people suffer and are allowed to suffer because Democracy allows and permits these 4 things to happen. But allow me to expand on the first point. Unemployment is a major issue in all societies. If being employed, gives life to a non-wealthy individual, therefore, being unemployed brings about the gradual decline of that person's life. In a world where money is king, a person without a job and losing whatever little he has may become desperate and willing to do anything to stay afloat. The moment a person becomes vulnerable in that sense is when that person becomes a danger to society.

Every one of the mishaps of the employee may spark the emergence of a new bad deed being done unto the people. The bottom line here is that the environment of the unrestricted world of Democracy provides the emergence of bad people, whereby it is not necessarily the fault of the bad people themselves that makes them bad in the first place but rather it is they who inflicted unto them a form of unfairness that are the ones to be at fault. (But because the law protects the employers who obey the law, although the employees feel a form of unfairness, there is nothing the employee can do other than to break down and cause societal disruptions because of his breakdown.)

There are also some rare cases where the employer is the victim of the employee(s). Or a more frequent case is where the employer is the victim of other employer(s) or the victim of employee(s) from another employer. In such cases, these evil deeds cause a ripple effect on the livelihoods of the members of society, and only the strong-minded in society are not influenced and retains their good societal values.

(It is for this reason that Socialism governs businesses and workplaces — to protect the people from the bad effects of allowing individuals from owning businesses. If we allow individuals to set up companies, we will have problems where members of society, end up getting trampled on and be unemployed. But through the state being in control of work, **if a good leader** is in power within the society, we may prevent unemployment and all forms of mistreatment towards the individual who **works in order to continue living**. The goal of Socialism is to be able to manage individuals so that society may continue existing in harmony. To achieve that, the system that we use is a system where every business and shop is owned by the state, this way we ensure that people across society, have a job and have a good enough pay.)

2. The Existence Of Scammers In Society

$\mathbf{T}$HE SOCIALISM THAT I have envisioned is one that does not allow scammers or the like to exist.

In Society, people can trick you into signing those 100-page contracts when purchasing houses. People can come to you and ask you to get insurance, where you end up paying for things that most of the time you won't need. And when the time comes for you to need them, they say that they do not cover that illness or that sort of injury and justice isn't available for you. There also exist cults where they take your money away and cause other societal disruptions. Scammers ask you to transfer money to them. Everywhere people are trying to get money from your account to their account. All this is happening in the world today, regardless of the government. The reason for this is because governments do not meddle closely into the lives of the people.

(The way I see it, governments lack the form of a justice system that cares for the individual that is not ruled by law but by conscience and values. Bluntly speaking, although quite unlikely to happen but, every democratic government lacks a King that is above the law, who is able to assess the situation correctly and bring about true justice.)

If a contract in which was signed by a person ends up tricking that person, when the issue is brought into the court of law, the person who is **tricked** into signing the contract in the first place, ends up getting the short end of the stick because he did sign the contract. Whatever reasoning he gives will fall upon deaf ears. But a leader who has a strong sense of justice and has the ability to defend the right of any person, won't allow this to happen this way.

What readers must know is **the law defends those who uphold the law regardless of their motive**. A person may have a bad motive but he will be protected by the law if he abides by the ways of the law as he executes that bad motive. The bad motive of the person itself ends up not being judged or taken into account. This is one of those fascinating problems that the world has, and no one conforming to democracy can solve this problem.

Once again I say this, Socialism cannot give you freedom. It can give you security and happiness but not freedom. Because the moment freedom is given, someone out there will use it to scam you, people will step on people. Freedom brings about many insecurities to those who are vulnerable. Freedom is the problem because people are prone to do evil to one another. This is human nature. This is the instinct found to exist within every human being. If religious people do not necessarily mean that they are good all the time, should we even allow freedom to anyone?

Let's get back to the original intent of this topic — the existence of scammers in society.

There are a variety of scammers in society but what is the main reason for scamming? It always comes down to money issues. Either because the person is currently jobless, or he is currently in need of money, or the current / previous job he undertakes has a low salary rate, or he was previously scammed and then decided to scam others, or he just wants to scam others to get richer because he is not happy with what little he currently has. Let me ask you, whose fault is it if a man finds himself in a low-paying job? Whose fault is it, whenever the world and the hardships therein, create a new scammer into existence? So from a hopefully shared point of view, the world creates the bad guy and the bad guy when he is caught is put behind bars by the government. Is this fair treatment, dear ladies and gentlemen? Can the government do anything in this case scenario? Not much, rather the hands of the government are tied by none other than Democracy itself.

The law is the one that puts the scammer behind bars no matter who it is or what it is that caused him to be bad in the first place. The law within Democracy, in other words, is heartless and is ignorant of the evils within society. The root of the problem is never solved in Democracy with regard to the existence of scammers and the money issues any individual may have in his life that may cause him to disturb, disrupt, or endanger the livelihoods of others. Life continues on for all people in Democracy without ease and without the protection from other **individual** members of society. I highlight the word individual because the government does handle groups of people that try to cause disruptions in society. But the evil works of the individual that is most of the time undetected, is never dealt with. Socialism believes that governments **must** get involved in the lives of their citizens because that's the only way to halt the root problems in society.

3. Joblessness & The Unemployed

A MAN WHO is jobless loses hope very quickly. It may not seem like it the first few days after he resigns. But if he intends to find another job while being jobless, a single problem that he faces or a misfortune that comes over him can turn him lifeless — which describes a man who has lost hope. What more miserable will he be if he does not have enough money to support himself for another month.

No matter how much care a President has upon his jobless citizens, the president can create jobs for them but would not be able to put them into a company that is already existing. To build a company for the unemployed to be able to work at is costly for the country. The ideal and most sufficient way is to direct the unemployed to existing companies. In reality, every company does not randomly choose their employees and so it is not possible even for the president to ask companies to accept and give wages to a random unemployed person and probably will have to break a couple of human rights laws to even do so.

In socialism, every company is owned by the state. The most ideal way to own every company is not to take over someone else's company but rather to build every single company and hence own them from the beginning.

And because the state owns the companies in it, it does not take long to get work for the unemployed. And as I have mentioned before, no one has to cry over their pitiful salaries because we make sure it is more than enough for you.

In a country with Democratic Leadership, it is not easy for those who are both unemployed and without a degree of study towards a particular field. Training or schooling should be able to be given unto them — those who want a job but do not have a degree at all.

Money makes the world go round. Without it, living becomes difficult even for the president who wants to be able to help people. He will not be able to help the people if the taxpayer's money is already completely being used by various programs that are either from past administrations or the one currently in place. What ends up happening if the president wants to help? I believe there are only 2 ways to do this and that is either to borrow money, to issue government bonds (which is an IOU that gives interest upon the return of the IOU bill to the one that issues it; for more about IOUs, kindly refer to '**Defining IOU Bills**' in the '**Supportive Definition References**' section), or to inflate the currency.

In socialism, money is not the most important thing. The normal logo of socialism is everyone holding hands forming a circle. Societal participation is what allows us to survive. Everyone has a role to play. Without farmers, we die. Socialism is about sustaining life. We depend on what we have. If we lose a particular occupation, society may fall apart. The creation and distribution of money to fellow citizens is easy for us. If financial is your most concerned problem in life despite all that is given to you in Democracy, meaning that if all you care about is to be financially secure and you would gladly trade that for everything else, Socialism is the cure. Money is this simple. The problem of survival in Socialism is Societal participation — whether individuals are willing to participate for the continual existence of the whole society or not.

People may speculate that what I speak is a joke because I say that money can be printed just like that. The thing is, if you print money based on societal participation (based on the wealth that is described by means of life — as long as societal participation does not stop, we all continue to have food on the table), you can print as much as you want and distribute it. The monetary system that I use is the same system you play Monopoly with. The paper money in that game cannot be used to purchase burgers from Burger King or coffee from Starbucks. It is only used inside the confines of the game itself. In my case, it is used inside the confines of the state. There is no exchange rate from the currency used to US Dollars or any other currency there exists today. Although the currency that the Socialist State uses is of no material value, it doesn't mean that your 1 US Dollar can purchase 10,000 burgers in the Socialist State. You will still have to change your US Dollars to the currency used inside the state and that exchange rate is only determined by our Socialist State without the analytical study of imports and exports. To simply put it, you have to purchase our currency to be able to buy inside our Socialist State; but we cannot purchase outside currency using our currency because no one trusts our currency to have value in the global market.

4. Society Molds Society

IF YOU ALLOW the ideology of a free country to do more or less anything, then the country will find itself molding up criminals that never existed in the early stages of a democratic ideology. Every society affects the lives and mental states of the people within it. A criminal will always have a cause for his actions. It is mostly because someone else did something to him. Whether it is through physical means or through a different means, it ends up hitting him in such a way he does crime. The more borderless the world is for people to get away by twisting laws and words to prevent them from being blamed as the wrong one, the crazier the criminals become. We have people who take the life of people they just met. I feel deeply saddened by the death of your loved ones but I cannot put the blame 100% on the killer. I have to put most of it really on the person who turned someone like you or me, into these heavily-burdened sad people who suddenly snap and end up doing the bad that they do. Usually, this happens to a society that lives under the democratic ideology.

I am sorry if I have to attack the democratic ideology this way. But the fact does remain that under an unsupervised society someone will get hurt by someone else's actions. And this sad world will blame the killer no matter what happened to him that causes him to snap. It is the society itself that allows that which that happened to him that causes him to snap.

This world that we live in is filled with profit-seeking people, it is filled with people holding to a variety of self-interests. The nature of these behaviors exists because of the system of the world. But what type of system is that? How did people become like this? We can all deduce that when society treats someone badly, society ends up molding that person to have certain characters, either his skin becomes thicker to endure, adapting to society whilst continue living peacefully with society or on the other extreme end, he becomes the next Hitler. That is an example of how the actions of a group of people mold certain characters in someone. But what about the problem where a child is born into society but without being bullied he becomes bad. Now in his case, it would be the fault of a flawed system. In other words, if a system is flawed, a child who grows up in that system will experience many bad things that did not happen to him because of the bad intentions of society but rather because society **have to** conform to that flawed system in order to live, causing the child to face bad experiences along the way **because** the system used, **dictates the definitions of life** to be like that.

We can agree that it is because of the difficulties of life that change boys to become real men but it feels like there is something amiss within this statement of truth. If this is how boys are shaped to become men, therefore those men may end up raising their children in the wrong way which will bring about a form of hatred from the children to their fathers. Not only will the children hate their own fathers but also will the children hate the fathers of their friends and loved ones, and do the same unto their own children just as how their fathers did unto them. Not just hatred will they have but other characters are also formed in the process of their growing up which may endanger society in the long run. They will keep on doing this and the ripple effect will continue, until one day they meet someone with good values and have their lives changed.

We come to the conclusion that a flawed system ends up dictating the definitions of life to be filled with troubles and only those who can conquer and navigate the waves of struggle are fit to live. This relates to the law of the jungle which is the survival of the fittest. This is not how

Democracy is seen by the people who promote it yet the ramifications of the flawed system that I have been talking about can be seen residing within the systems of Democracy.

5. Surface Problems Are Connected To Other Unseen Problems

IT IS NOT possible and adequate for us to fix just the current problem. We have to fix the problem from its roots. In other words, we have to fix the foundations first which led to the current problem. Maybe a social norm led to the problem although the problem has nothing to do with human social activities. It is difficult to ensure that fixing the current problem will definitely solve the problem. Because the cause that led to the problem may have no direct connection that most intellectuals could think of. Therefore the best way is to rewrite the foundation from the start with restrictions. If that doesn't work, we should rewrite the foundation again by either changing or adding restrictions because there must have been something that was skipped or that there might have been something that we missed out given our understanding at that point in time.

Imagine a serial killer being asked a question, why does he do it? If he were to seriously search within himself and do not understand the reasoning himself, he would tell you a story. A normal human being is asked to describe himself. But because he doesn't know much about himself or feels that there isn't much to tell or he doesn't understand how to convey it, the only way he would convey it to you is by telling you a story. A psychologist asks a person a yes or no question. And the person couldn't find the words to say it. And even if he were to say it, it wouldn't make sense to himself and so rather than saying that he doesn't know, he told the psychologist a story starting from his childhood which is seen as irrelevant to the question but is actually very relevant. The reason people go towards using a story to answer a yes or no question is to help the person asking, to lead them to an understanding about himself, he has to describe a detailed story of his life. After which, the person asking could understand him, but that understanding may not be completely correct either due to the fact that it is an understanding received through a verbal told description. People could get it right, people could get it wrong.

Likewise is it with the problems of the economy today. It is difficult for us to fix the current problem because that problem may be connected to human behavior, social norms, cultural change. I believe that things are connected and a problem arises in society because of wrong mixtures of variables.

Why do I give this lecture on connection? Because I am sure people will say to me that we could just fix the problem and that we do not have to reinvent civilization.

People will say to me, "Just give me your ideas and we will integrate them into the current situation, and it will fix the problem without your Socialist ideology that institutes restrictions to the masses." Let me say it once again. It won't work. You can't overlay another system above an existing system not because there is a problem with the integration process but because there is a problem not connected to it. There is a missing factor that you are overseeing that will lead to either a failed system or lead to the same problem today. The problem is similar to this. A man who is addicted goes into rehabilitation but the moment he gets out, he goes back to his addiction. Addiction may not be the problem. I am saying the problem will somehow persist unless we rebuild society. Reshaping it isn't going to work.

Allow me to add another paragraph. The most important factor in coexistence is the moral values within the members. When we reshape a society, what we are trying to do is asking them to change. Asking people to change does not ensure that they will change. We can force them but forcing is not a good idea because, as I said, **the step-by-step process** by which an end result is achieved somehow **will affect** the end result itself. A forceful process will reach a result where people may become resistant and rebellious in the future. That's not what we want. And so the best way is, the dream of Socialism, to reinvent society from the ground up so that people have an understanding of societal contributions and coexistence even from the city building process. It is from the city building process that those who participate in it understand what coexistence relates to.

6. Other Social Problems

DEPRESSION IS MOSTLY about one's economy going downwards. But that doesn't need to happen under a self-sustaining economy (used by early Socialist communities) — an economic system that does not rely on another country but mainly on itself can prevent the people from thinking what if(s), what if(s), what if(s). All that the people will be doing is to live their lives every day without much of any problems because we provide a means of work, we ensure a viable payday and the things that are both consumable and non-consumable, that which you may need, the state provides for you. No longer will you need to think about bank loans, house bills or rent, or housing itself. No longer a need to think of a way to sustain your life because as long as you can work or as long as we could provide a job for you, and we actually have the law where everyone must work, we make sure that you are paid well for your services to society, enough for you to feed a family of four. And because we want a society that lasts, you work less than or equal to 30 hours a week and there are quite a number of other benefits that we give you.

Another word troubling society is 'impatient'. Impatient itself causes many social problems. Cutting queues has become a norm in some parts of the world. When people feel that they are at a loss of time, they become self-centered people. And self-centered people do injure the people around them. The question is what causes them to be impatient? (1) The wicked world around them may sponsor this characteristic trait — because someone did one bad thing to them, they do the same bad thing or something different to someone else, (2) having the feeling of being pressured by someone else / not wanting to be horned at / wanting to be seen as someone capable — these come under the category of being pressured. And lastly, (3) the increase in technology that provides everything to be fast. When a person lives in a world where its fast and one day decides to take his bike for a spin and comes into a traffic jam, it becomes a problem because he will get impatient real fast and try to squeeze his bike in between cars which may damage one of the cars in a traffic jam. People who are impatient will turn into people who are ignorant of the loss they themselves might cause to someone else.

How do societies break down? The way I see it, it starts with economic hardships. The income the family gets is either just right, a little bit above just right, or below just right whereas they cannot cope with the spending for their needs. Business competition comes along, employee wages fluctuate, people get removed from jobs. In practice, I have heard people talking that these people who lose jobs will in the coming months or a year later receive some line of work to feed themselves. But what was overlooked was not whether they will get jobs or not but during their waiting period, what happens to their mind, their heart or their self. A man who is currently in his productive age has to wait for 6 to 9 months before getting another job. Now, we don't know what sort of things could happen to him. He may get depressed, he may try or think to take his life, he may be pressured by family, he may start drinking, he may start gambling, he may produce fits of anger on a daily basis. Even if he succeeds to get a job after 9 months, these things that have happened to him, his mental changes, or irrational behavior changes, may affect other people around him. All this, just because a young man starts a business that creates a sort of competition with older companies in his neighborhood. Without restrictive laws that could prevent such an outcome on human society, it becomes a maddening situation.

Loneliness is another problem in today's society. With much social interaction every day, we could ensure individualism doesn't happen. Loneliness produces a rise in suicide cases and other probable social problems. And so I need society to have the interactions needed in daily life. People need to interact with people, their co-workers for example. To ensure this, people need jobs and we have to force people to work at least 4 hours a day. To ensure this stays that way we have restrictions on wealth. A man can be rich but he still has to work as long as he is under the pension age, which has a set of rules to follow. That man can buy stuff for his son but he cannot transfer money to his son's account except upon his death, that too has a set of rules to follow.

All our restrictions are placed not for the sole purpose of preventing or prisoning people from a better life. Every person will have a good life if the society, they are in, exists tomorrow. If that society dies tomorrow, it will affect all peoples within it.

An example is this. A young man who inherits a lot of money tends to be lazy to work. If he goes about telling people of this restriction while not understanding the wisdom behind the restriction that prevents society to die tomorrow, he will have followers. With followers, the lives of the people living in that society become endangered in the long run. The society that lasts is the society that remains socially connected and the way I built the society is that we support one another by working, by socializing, by helping one another. I do my job, and you do your job to support society, to be a part of society. Everyone works to live. Those that have abundant savings and those that do not, continue to work despite what they have. Together, we support one another. If a man becomes lazy and he stops working and if the state ignores him, others will become lazy to the point where farmers become lazy and then we all die due to having no food at the table.

When I first envisioned a city for the people, I started with a moneyless society where a person can go to a bakery shop and ask for any bread and receives it. He can get 10 bread, no questions asked. The problem is, people are greedy, they are lazy, they have problems with being honest, they have problems with only taking what they need. It becomes a problem, that is why I have to issue paper money that will be obtained through jobs.

Because what I see happening is, the state purchases 50 pianos from Germany. These are Grand Pianos which are really expensive. And because we purchase it using Germany's currency and not for free, we have to sell our crops or products to them to get their currency and then be able to purchase the 50 pianos. Now a man who lives alone in a house comes to the piano store and maybe out of wickedness or selfishness, gets 10 of these pianos into his house. Now if you are able to see the problem that is happening here, my reasoning to issue paper money checks out. There are other problems that arise because of human beings and their evil hearts or their own human nature that will cause problems if I do not issue the paper money obtainable through jobs.

These restrictions that are placed onto the socialist state are restrictions that try to prevent the evil or wickedness in the human heart to be brought out into actions that will certainly cause hurt to other people. If the restrictions are not placed, humans will by nature eventually hurt other humans. When there is nothing to restrain people, people tend to yearn for more. "If I could be better or richer or have more free time than him, then why not." This mentality is not bad. It is just not good to have this mentality if we want to live amongst others. To be able to live with the people around us, so that society does not tear itself apart, we need to be attentive towards others. A lasting society demands a form of caring from each and every one of us, for it to really last. Striving to be better will help society but wanting to have more or be more than others deteriorate ones' wisdom.

A cycle may happen and the good we want may not last. Because a wise man may teach his children the wisdom he begets from experience and the children will receive that information in the form of an understanding. And many years later as that understanding is being passed down from generation to generation, humans who are curious by nature will tend to challenge that understanding and because they will succeed at first for the first 50 years at what they thought about, people will then forget about the understanding that they have received and when society fails again, the cycle begins another round.

Because wisdom is information received through experience — this cannot be challenged by those who have this wisdom whereas understanding is information not begot through experience. And wisdom is achieved and understood through the survival of hardships but the people living in the cities will not be living in hardships. This brings us to the only way out will be to make a rule that states that the ideology will not change in the future. If someone wants to challenge the ideology, may they do it on top of another piece of land, from scratch, so that this working system, that has been built, does not end up being disrupted.

7. Final Remarks On The Past Six Sub-Chapters

WE ARE BROUGHT to the conclusion that Democracy and the workings of Democracy that shape the society, is a flawed system. It lacks love and attention, it allows society to be shaped in a wrong way which hinders the conquest of good societal values. Ultimately, it lacks a personal relationship with members of its society.

V. Imposing Democracy Unto The World

DEMOCRACY HAS BEEN imposed upon countries all over the world. There is an unseen plot of turning the world into being filled with Democratic countries. We know that somehow Democracy has knocked at the doors of every country, trying to get itself into those countries, lest be branded as a country that does not recognize freedom to be given unto its people. And it is also by means of pitching the idea to the people itself, causing an insurgence by the people, demanding for Democracy. I am very sure that many will view this topic as a theory of conspiracy — seen as something that can't be an agenda coming from human beings. As was previously given the information thereof, within every Democracy lies Capitalist ideology. In fact, the freedom allowed in Democracy is used by people (who are able to see and exploit the flaw) as a helping hand towards their agendas — the agendas of the unjust, greedy, and evil.

Democracy is supposed to allow the freedom of values. Yet it forces its way into almost all of the world's countries. The big question here is why? What is the reason for the need of Democracy to extend its ideas and ideals to exist within other countries? Who profits from this expansion? To answer that we must dig up a couple of ridiculous truths that Democracy brings about.

What regular people understand is that Democracy has a good goal which is to give forms of Freedom to the inhabitants of the country. Religion, especially Christianity in America gives cheer to the idea of Democracy dominating the world. But the regular people and Christians themselves are unable to see that there is an agenda of profit and power that can be done towards a country that allows Democratic ideals to enter its walls. In other words, these two groups or more only see the sales pitch of Democracy and happily drive it forward but behind the scenes, there is a sinister plot that is pro-business, a plot of self-interest is present. Business brings profit. Profit brings power. Power brings control. If every country opens up itself economically, and also allows itself to enter into world markets, then theoretically speaking, any country has the probability of being economically controlled by other countries or even persons.

People may not be aware that the most powerful entity in any given country is not the government in most cases. Those who have power are businessmen — people who have a lot of paper money which also means that they hold a big percentage of the wealth of the country that paper money represents. (This is why I hold to the view that paper money becomes problematic if people do not see it as paper that brings about a formal consistent form of barter but rather sees it as wealth itself. Because those who see paper money as wealth itself and not created as a means for society to do trade with one another, which are two very different things, will end up keeping paper money and those who are evil will not just keep paper money but see it as power and as the evil grows within themselves corrupting the person in such a way that he uses money to have control over others.)

We all know that in ancient times, the king is the one who has the most power. The king has power and authority, he creates laws and makes decisions. Even merchants bow down to kings. But in our modern world, this is not the case. In our time today, businessmen or very rich people are the ones who are seen to have power. When our governments need money, they go to people who have the money; they make deals with people who have money (most of which are never disclosed to the people).

With all this in mind, our countries today allow individuals to have power because of the number of paper money that they own. (In my own understanding, to allow this is wrong. Because there is no chance for sure to know that people will not use power any way they like; it is wrong to allow individuals to have power. In fact, listen to this statement : if a system allows the ability where someone is able to do something bad to someone else, that system should not be implemented. A system is only known to be good if no one can sabotage the life of others within it.) So we live in a world where power is in the hands of individuals, which opens the door to many evil motives. And when you have a lot of something, people tend to challenge themselves to see how far they can go by trying to accumulate more of that something. This is the world we live in, ladies and gentlemen. That is why people like myself show up to tackle Capitalism and its many followers that hide behind Democracy who at the same time try to profit using Democracy, whether they know it or not (whether being done consciously or unconsciously) which ends up causing hurt in its many forms to societies of the world.

This whole topic almost sounds like a fantasy — something not possible to be currently taking place in our societies. But one of the facts is that we live in a world where anyone can amass wealth and wealth being represented by paper money is seen by this age (this current world) we live in, as power.

But let us now return to discussing the ridiculous truths that Democracy brings about. We have currently side-tracked quite a bit towards the knowledge of individuals having seen to have more power or has the ability to be above the government because of paper money and its wrong allowed usage thereof.

One of those truths that I am talking about is that Democracy brings about the freedom of trade between countries and also gives way so that foreign businesses may enter into the country. This forces countries to open their doors for outsiders to enter their markets and also obtain **resources** (eg. natural resources, trees, gold, oil reserves, etc.), that were previously unobtainable. In other words, by asking others to conform to Democratic values, behind the scenes it was to make the countries vulnerable to be exploited by.

In other words, individuals in a country want something from other countries, and the only way to obtain it is by bringing the idea of Democracy to those countries.

Other ridiculous truths surround the fact that Democracy has been molded into a system that is exploitable by people who know how. And those individuals take up the opportunity given to them to excel and become and have more than others.

The reason the rules of religion, the statutes of God, were made to enter into the life of individuals in a restrictive manner, is to prevent self-interest; it is to have the individuals love their neighbor. If God is good then He would want His people to be good. Goodness cannot be accomplished by free will alone or by being given the freedom to do what you want. Goodness can only be accomplished if the values of the individual conform to the understanding of the same goodness that goodness itself represents. Democracy brings free will to the table but free will itself does not ensure evil people do not exist. Therefore as good human beings, early Socialists try to think up of ways to eradicate self-interest which gave birth to Socialism — the best system a human being can think of that is fair and just.

VI. Democracy & Representative Governments

ASIDE FROM FREEDOM, what else does Democracy bring unto its citizens? Supposedly fair elections and decisions, that are thought to be made by a majority vote. But once a president has been elected by a majority vote, whatever he / she does afterward, no longer depends on a majority vote. In other words, the public only has a say on who becomes president. Whatever the president chooses to do, no longer is determined by a majority vote.

It's quite funny that the voices of the people no longer means anything once the election is over in a Democracy. Although peaceful demonstrations are done, it is only on few occasions that Governments listen to the objections of the people. Maybe governments believe that those who do not show up in demonstrations are those who agree with whatever decisions the government makes. But that's not totally true. Most of the time people are just not willing to stand under the beating sun that may suddenly change into the pouring of rain.

In the communities of Socialism, the views of individuals matter. It is a requirement of the leader to listen to the problems that his people are facing — the people could voice out their complaints, or seek to understand the reasoning behind certain laws and why those laws must be present. The state which oversees all the activities within the society is who the people have to go to directly if they want or need something. The state does not just solve problems of the state, like the restocking of foreign goods, or solve a problem in the energy sector. But the state also solves the problem of needs and wants from individual people. The people also can go to the state to offer an idea, or to ask for the availability of Mexican foods to exist in a particular district or ask for an ice-skating rink, or request to go to Russia or other countries for vacation. It may sound a bit off to ask governments to do something for you in a Democracy, but in a Socialist environment, where the existence of the state is to make happy the people, every individual's plea to meet with the state, is the right given to the individual. It is the duty of the state to try its best to accommodate the wishes of the people. In the event it cannot, reasoning will be provided.

Democratic governments care for the country. They care for the economy of the country. They care for the stability of the country as a whole. Democracy worries about the food crisis, the country is facing. Democracy tends to the problems faced by **the majority** of its people. I do not know if the readers can detect the problems in Democratic governments found in this paragraph but the problems are right there in plain sight.

What is a country, do you know? What does it consist of? A landmass consisting of people on the surface of that landmass. Yes, but what does a person mean when he says he cares for his country? Does he truly care for all the inhabitants of the country or does he mean that he just cares for the majority of it? Is it as long as that landmass and the number of people on that landmass, constitute as being known as a country, he cares for the country? If that is the case, how many people does he care for if he says he cares for his country?

Democratic countries care for the economy of their country. This does not mean that they care for the economy of the individuals of the country. These are two different things. Another mentioned thing is what problems are quelled by the government and what is not quelled.

The way I see it, governments just don't understand that the happiness of every individual actually matters and is of importance for the well-being of the whole country. They just assume that if the majority is pleased, if the problems of the majority are quelled, they have done a great job. This is so untrue. Taking care of the majority does something yes but what about the minority? If tomorrow a person from that minority sets off a bomb somewhere, will the government put the blame on itself or will the government judge the person whom the government didn't care for previously?

Maybe people are wondering, can the writer envision a government that is capable of taking care of everyone without exceptions? My answer is yes but we will have to reinvent civilization first. We need to build a city from the ground up and then set up the rules and system of Socialism as its foundations. Then place a government body that oversees all the activities of the city and who strongly cares for the people. After that fill up the city with people found around the globe who wants to be freed from financial problems and are in need of a roof above their heads, comfort, and stability in life. Finally, let the state do the rest.

VII. Comments On Grand Chapter : Democracy

SADLY THIS IS all I have about Democracy. My whole point concerning Democracy is that if the reader were to inspect carefully the societies living under Democracy, you will find all these problems in society be present because of the unseen nature of what Freedom brings about.

Evil or bad motivations come from the heart. We don't get to know who is bad or who is good by appearances. And because evil people are made evil, **something** made them evil. Either the ways of the society makes one evil or evil is self-motivated by desires like greed, whichever it is, something happened to that person.

According to some studies, justice and fairness are found in children. But as we grow into adults and start to have wants and dreams, during that growing up process we become selfish, self-centered, and have an ego. But once we reached adulthood or once we become mature, studies say that only a few obtained wisdom in such a way that they choose not to retain those bad character traits.

Although religion also plays a part in shaping our values, evil still somehow manages to spread because of a lack of a strong moral conscience in addition to an environment of freedom. In the end, people who live good honest lives get harmed (get disturbed / get influenced / being shown injustice to / being seen as unimportant / get stepped on / be cheated / be financially discriminated / be harmed financially, etc.) by people with various motives. It all comes down to the fact that Democracy does not suppress evil intent.

The title of this book is 'Preferring Socialism Over Democracy : Envisioning Cities Of Societal Harmony & Continual Coexistence'. Because Socialism allows restrictive laws to enter the lives of the individual, having the right laws could suppress evil intent. It may be a shocker to some readers who may be expecting the talk between Socialism and Democracy to be about political issues or about high-level complicated stuff, whereas my fight against Democracy is simple and more towards the values that the people within society are made to have and may be forced to adapt to. In fact, Socialism isn't attacking Democracy but rather attacking the existence of Evil itself, trying to suppress it from its roots which come from human actions towards their fellow neighbor.

People go everywhere to find solutions to their problems. Little do they know that the solution is found within every individual and their moral values as a collective to society. Bring about the right values in every individual and then every other individual will have a promising future. And the best way to do this is not by forcing the people to have good values but through a difficult long-winding process of giving people the understanding while ensuring that the understanding is understood as a good thing. (Life itself gives you an understanding by repetition, whether you understood what the best way to live is, comes back to the person living it.) There are short-cuts that can be done to achieve this but it is wise to allow the human being to use his own free will to choose the right values, having been given the understanding thereof.

[May the reader understand that Socialism is not an ideology that forces itself unto people but rather seeks to build a place where people can live and grow together. It yearns for the people, who choose to live within its walls, to have an understanding of good societal culture that intends to bring about continual societal co-existence. Once again, true Socialism does not bring itself upon an already existing society that carries a different ideology but rather seeks to build a society from scratch that has Socialist values as its foundations.]

Democracy gives freedom to both sides. Because we cannot detect the good from the bad, what we need is a leader with good values that uses a restrictive system that restricts both the good and the bad from bringing about evil into society. That summarizes the preference for Socialism over Democracy.

Final Conclusion : Socialism is a good system **only if** the leader is a good person because the leader will instruct the people how to live and if the leader is good therefore the people are forced to live and be good, whereas Democracy is a good system **only if** the people within it are good people and having good values. Which one does the reader think is easier of being realized in the real world?

THIRD GRAND CHAPTER :
BUILDING SOCIALISTIC CITIES &
ITS ENVISIONED GUIDELINES

Preferring Socialism Over Democracy :
Envisioning Cities Of Societal Harmony &
Continual Coexistence

Mini Intro

THIRD GRAND CHAPTER :
BUILDING SOCIALISTIC CITIES &
ITS ENVISIONED GUIDELINES

PREVIOUSLY WE TALKED about Socialism, Democracy, and many Definitions. With the three, I have given why readers should prefer Socialism over Democracy and knowledge of how society can be harmonized. What readers will find here is further knowledge of harmonizing and how future Socialistic cities would be built.

I have written the following first by giving what society will be like within Socialism, followed by how the city would most likely be built and populated. Also, not to mention, how paper money will be issued and how the inhabitants will live within it.

I. The Monetary System Used In Socialism

THIRD GRAND CHAPTER :
BUILDING SOCIALISTIC CITIES &
ITS ENVISIONED GUIDELINES

A SOCIALIST SOCIETY is dependent on the existence of the society itself. In this society, each and every person has a job that they do as part of society. They do jobs that the community has deemed a societal job — a job required by society in order that the society itself can both exist and function continually.

If everyone knows their part to play in a Socialist society and they live for the continual existence of the society as directed by the needs of society, paper money does not need to exist in the first place. People can just go to the restaurant (which is state-owned) and order their food and drinks, they can go to a bakery or ice-cream shop (also state-owned) and take their choice bread and ice-cream, without needing to go to the cashier.

But people can and do change with time. People can become lazy over time. The next generation may try not working and yet eat what they want, and see what happens. As Socialists, we try to identify the problem before it even happens. We do not wait for it to happen first and then do something about it. We are meticulously detailed when it comes to planning our cities and economic systems. After we identify the problems that could surface, we search for the root cause and then restrict the root cause from ever happening. Because people may become lazy to go to work since they get free food anyway, paper money is issued to the public by the state as a means of prevention towards a future societal breakdown. But this paper money that is issued by the Socialist government is different from the ones issued in free democratic countries.

Paper money as the world knows it to be, represents a form of value that is fixed in the amount of wealth. But the paper money that is issued inside an already-working Socialist society (that doesn't actually need paper money in the first place) does not represent anything. If it represents anything at all, it would be the existential existence of society itself. As long as society continues to exist, the paper money issued in the Socialist environment will retain its value no matter the amount in circulation. This is the famously mocked Socialist understanding of printing money out of thin air without causing inflation. This understanding is mocked by the intellectuals of the world because they do not understand what we mean when true Socialists say that they can print money without causing inflation.

In order for you to print money without inflation, you first need a working society where every single person understands and works for the sake of the existence of society. They understand that success is achieved when everyone plays their part in society and therefore one indirectly cares for one another through partaking in society. After you have a working Socialist society where the society can feed itself and function continually, only then can you print money as a means to prevent laziness and give wages to all the working people in society and setup prices within shops in such a way that people will continue to work for the existence of society itself.

In the history of the world, there are people who call themselves Socialists and believe that they can print money out of thin air. These people end up causing hyperinflation to the economy of their country. Although they call themselves Socialists, they do not understand the mindset of Socialism. That is why in the previous chapters, I differentiate between people who read about Socialism and like the idea of Socialism, with people who are born under the star of Socialism where their personality is a Socialist personality. I have to differentiate them and give that understanding to the reader because it really matters a lot what defines a true Socialist so that people do not hate Socialism because of all the false Socialism in existence in our modern world.

II. Full-Time Jobs & Wages

THIRD GRAND CHAPTER :
BUILDING SOCIALISTIC CITIES &
ITS ENVISIONED GUIDELINES

EVERY PERSON IN a Socialist society must have a full-time job. That is the only way the collective society will accept him / her to live within society. Whether the person is a rich person or has a rich parent, that individual must choose a full-time job to do. This is one of the rules of societal coexistence. And every work done is compensated by means of a base salary (based on the living standards of one obese person) and an extra salary that is based on the contributions that job does for society & how many people it affects on a daily basis. This may imply that whatever job that the world wages low in their societies (eg. farmers, construction workers, caretakers, etc.) may be paid well, within a socialist society.

Usually, in a Socialist society, the state may require a job to be filled because society needs someone to do that job in order for the society to function (maybe an issue came up and we are in urgent need of people in a particular field). In such a case, the state may add extra wages for that needed job and promote it to people with the skills to do the job for a period of time. Therefore a wage consists of a basic wage, and layers of extra wages, depending on what he / she does for the collective society.

In the event that a person wants to do a job but does not have qualifications, the state may help him to get his dream job. This is one of the pros of having a good state own every business and company in the society — they have the power to give people any job they currently yearn to do.

No matter what a person has done for the collective society, even if the person has 10 layers of extra wages because of the contributions that have been contributed, he still is required to have a full-time job. But rest assured, the full-time job (for anyone in the socialist society) takes lesser than that of the 8 hours a day and 40 hours a week system being used by the world.

III. Ownership In Socialism : Business & Property

BLUNTLY SPEAKING, private ownership of business, houses, landmass, and transportation is not allowed. Although it may sound unpleasant, there is wisdom behind these restrictions.

The land within the confines of the city belongs to the collective society. Allowing a person to be able to buy land, gives him the power to rob that land from the collective society. Allowing a person to purchase land also gives him the power to sell it. There is a saying that says that it is the seller that sets the price. Given that there is a probability that the buyer will buy as much land as he can as a means to hoard land masses, and the seller may sell the land to gain more profit, in order to prevent both these people with bad intentions to the collective society (which should consist of

189

loving and caring people towards one another) from appearing in society, any landmass is disallowed to be owned by any individuals. Every landmass in this case will only belong to the state for the use of the collective society. Whether it is to build housing, recreational areas, entertainment grounds, factories, or public services, it would be used only to profit the collective society.

Transportation is also an issue if it is allowed to be bought by individuals. When people are allowed to buy any vehicle from the state, they end up being given the ability to use it, without ever repairing it. A used car tends to have problems and some people are ignorant of the problem as long as it does not affect oneself. This mindset is a problem for the collective society. Although not every person is evil, evil intent exists and can be prevented only by restricting all of society. But if the collective owns transportation as a whole, therefore for the well-being of the collective itself, checks and repairs will be made annually, financed by the state, also acting as a means to create jobs. We do hope that society will be diligent at the jobs when they know that they are doing it for the sake of the collective which includes, they themselves.

For housing, it is also as a means of preventing any evil intent of citizens towards their fellow citizens. In a working Socialist society, every person or family will be given a form of default housing by the state based on their family count. A newly married couple will also be given a default housing fit for them. These default housing should be free unless they want an upgrade that does not reflect their current family count, in which case they would need to pay extra costs for a house that fits more than their family count. As for the insides of the house, the furniture, decorations, kitchen set, these can be owned by the individuals.

As for private ownership of businesses, this is to prevent the evils that can be done from an employer to the employee, like giving unfair wages, dictating working hours, disregarding health and the safety of their employees, etc. Private ownership of businesses is also not allowed because it may lead to competition amongst businesses doing the same trade. What we do allow is if there is an idea for a business or cooking recipe or story writing, or entertainment creations, those with ideas can come to the state and present it to the state. If we deemed it to be something that can profit the collective society or is useful to it, whatever your idea is, the state will accommodate it and you may gain extra wages to add to the wages you receive for your full-time job.

These are the reasons for the restrictions on private ownership of things within society. Having these restrictions incorporated into law does not imply the state to be above the people but rather by doing so, the state serves the collective society by imposing restrictions for the sake of societal harmony.

IV. Trade Amongst Countries Or Cities

HOW WILL TRADE be done between a Socialist society with other countries or cities? Before I answer that question, does the reader know how it is currently being done from a country to another country?

When we are talking about trade, we are referring to two terminologies. The trade of the individual or business, and the trade that is done by the government, both of which are done with businesses, individuals, or governments of other countries. But how can the currency of country A be of value to a person in country B? If country A's currency is seashells and country B's currency is starfishes and both these countries do not value the other country's currency, how do they do trade with one another? That is the question we want to know the answer to.

In modern society, trade is currently being done by means of currency exchange rates. What happens is when a person in country A wants to buy something in country B is as follows. Behind the scenes, following the example of seashells and starfishes, first, the person in country A, buys the starfishes of country B using his seashells. Then he uses the starfishes (which is the currency of country B) to do business with the person in country B. All these are done in a moment of seconds by the currency exchange market.

The currency exchange market calculates the prices of every currency in the world. This global system calculates the value of every currency, based on the exports and imports of the country in real-time. Because of the complexity of the calculations, some people believe that the calculations themselves are non-existent and that the exchange market is a hoax altogether that values a currency based on the wants of a group of elite bankers.

I would like the reader to read the topic of "**Defining The Fluctuations Of A Country's Currency**" within the '**Supportive Definition References**' Section of this book for more information about the currency exchange market also before continuing to the next paragraph in order to be able to understand **points (1) & (2)** found there.

As for the issue of this current topic of discussion, trade from a Socialist society is as the following. Selling excess food and energy is the main way for us to do trade with other countries. We also do trade through selling the goods and services we have created within the society to other countries in order to obtain their currency. Once we have their currency, we (the state, on behalf of the society and not the individual citizen themselves) then purchase whatever we need that is needed or wanted by our Socialist society. By doing it this way, (1) we do not unconsciously or consciously take back any of their paper money which may cause a scarcity of it in their country because we could make sure to spend all their paper money before exiting their country, (2) because of point 1, this causes a **balance** in the export-import of that country in such a way that the currency of the country we do trade with remains the same value in the currency exchange market; if there are changes, it will not be because of us, (3) as a means to make it much clearer to the reader, the economy of that country will be as though we were never there.

Point 2 in the previous paragraph where is stated that the export and import are balanced, this balancing has always been the dream of world economists for the economy. They have always hoped that one day, the monthly exports and imports are balanced so that the economy of every country will not fluctuate. This is an ideal economy, world economists wanted for the world, which I believe can never be achieved using the current trade system done using direct currency exchange.

Yes, the Socialist way of trade between countries is a complicated old-fashion way of doing trade. And because it is the state that does the trade for the people in society, this becomes much easier to manage (once again as long as the leader of the Socialist State & the government body are good guys). But as can be seen by the reader, there are pros of trade to be done in this manner compared to the current manner it is being done through currency exchange.

So you might be asking: if the state is the only one that does trade with other countries, does this mean that individual people do not have the freedom to buy foreign goods? What can be done is this. For example, a person wants furniture from IKEA which is not found in our society. We would then ask him or her what he or she wants from IKEA. Then the (good) state will open up a purchasing order for the collective. Because the state cannot afford to go to and fro on a daily basis, we collect the wants of the people and then do trade directly with IKEA by going to the country where IKEA is found and purchasing the wants of the people there. Of course, IKEA will be notified first so that they could make ready the list of goods upon our arrival.

Before we depart to buy the goods, we will set up a price list with regard to the currency used by society. Once the person has paid the amount that was set by the state concerning the goods to be purchased, then the state proceeds with plans to depart to fulfill the wants of the people. So the people do not receive it for free but will have to purchase it with the wages the state gave them for their participation towards the continual existence of society. Of course, the getting-the-money part from the country we intend to buy from would be a complicated process, but the state will serve the people on that matter without fail.

V. Side Pastimes, Ideas & Creative Creations By Citizens In Socialist Societies

Third Grand Chapter : Building Socialistic Cities & Its Envisioned Guidelines

PEOPLE MAY HAVE dreams, they may have ideas, they may like to create things in their free time. The Socialist State, because it is also a state that finds ways to make happy the people, it needs a form of value that can be exchanged to receive the currency of other countries when they need to purchase goods from those countries. This is where the individual citizen's creativeness may come in to help the collective society. We tend to find products or services that can be sold to other countries by means of our citizens and their ideas. We do not force the citizens to share it with us, but if they are willing to help the collective, we could accommodate their dreams and at the same time use it as value for trade with other countries.

What are the things that an enclosed socialist society can use in order to obtain some form of value that can be exchanged with the currencies of other countries and nations (for the sole purpose of trade)?

Entertainment and content from artists, actors, movies, music, plays, musician, orchestra, painters & paintings, writers & books. Ideas for technological, services, software, or innovative products like designs for better transportation, researching other forms of clean energy, creating games & apps, innovative products for kitchenware, or multi-function furniture designs.

These are ideas that could be turned into usable products or create entertainment for both the socialist society and can be also sold to other countries with regard to the popularity of the product. Useful products or popular artists could become famous in the outside world (through the help of the state) if they can show their popularity within the socialist societies. These will allow more things to be bought by the collective society. People may see this as a means to exploit one's own talent for the happiness of the collective. But the reader must understand once again that, the people who become residents of a Socialist society, live and work for the collective society by their own free will. They know that society cares for them as a collective and so they may choose to still share their ideas even though the collective society will end up being happier than compared to the talented individuals who gave their idea in the first place.

But rest assured, because it would be unfair to not reward the person who gave the idea for the happiness of society as a whole, the person will also be compensated well.

VI. Restrictions & Laws Concerning Money & Its Socialist Design

As WRITTEN PREVIOUSLY that in Socialistic societies, money is created (physically or digitally) as a means to prevent laziness from individuals in society. Because Socialism is a society where many restrictions are found, the reader may be surprised it also does have restrictions towards personal income and how the person will be able to use it for.

Concerning the flow of money. Every business is owned by the state. This makes every citizen an employee of the state and is waged by the state. When a person enters a shop to buy goods or services, once he uses the money at the cashier and gives it over, the moment it is given over, the value of money given becomes void. This means that when the money exchanges hand, from one citizen towards another, it no longer has any value at the other person's hand. Because money was created to prevent laziness, the moment it is used one time, its existence has to vanish. This prevents a form of loophole for evil to be done in the system. Money becomes like how coupons are used. When the coupon has been used at a shop, the coupon is punctured and no other person can buy using a punctured coupon. The best way to utilize this is to use digital money instead of physical money.

There also won't be such a thing as the ability to transfer money from one person to the next, whether it is a friend or family member. This is to prevent the possible use for evil to be done towards a fellow citizen.

In Democracy, laws do not enter the livelihoods of the citizen because it believes that the conscience of a human being will not allow themselves to harm other people. But in Socialist ideologies, because a man's conscience can be crooked or a man's heart can be wicked, it is best to not allow mankind to make the choices based on his choosing but instead disallow the man from doing whatever the leader believe is bad. This makes the system to be based on the precepts of the leader. If the leader is God, then the system is good. If the leader is the incarnate of the evil one, then the system is bad.

Continuing onwards, the best way for a Socialist society to issue money to its people is to also allow children who attend schools to have a bank account where they too are paid by the state to go to school. So both the working people of society and the studying children of society are waged by the state. Of course, a parent can buy things for their child and also vice-versa the child can buy stuff for their parents but the transfer of money between one to another will not be allowed.

Because society exists due to the existence and cooperation of everyone in society, therefore the **basic wage** of every individual is not a small amount but an amount suited for one person. Because we value every person within a Socialist environment, every person is compensated well for their presence in society. As long as the society is a society that can feed itself and as longs as the existence of society is functional, the basic wage given will be a grand enough wage for one person. The reader must always keep in mind that money is present only as a means to fight off laziness and everything is done to accommodate it under the wisdom and mindset of Socialism.

VII. Viewing A Socialist State As A Family

THIRD GRAND CHAPTER :
BUILDING SOCIALISTIC CITIES &
ITS ENVISIONED GUIDELINES

THE SOCIALIST STATE is a state of families living together forming a huge family, one helping the other. The Socialist Governing body is the head of the family and as the head of any family, it is the duty of the head to ensure economic stability for the family. In other words, it is the duty of the father to provide for his children. Under a normal family, the children do not need to know about money. They receive whatever the head of the family gives them. When we were children ourselves, we do not need the understanding of money and wages. We know not the value of a thousand-dollar bill. We just live our lives caring for one another. Our respective fathers are the ones working to provide for the family. This is how I see the Socialist cities that I envisioned, to be.

When the children reach adulthood, they will begin to understand the workings of their father. In a normal family, the father who owns a business is then helped by his grown-up children to expand the business and hopefully provide more for the family and their future generations.

The envisioned Socialist State is a huge family where each member gets to choose either to serve one another (by doing paying jobs that give services to their society example: waitresses, construction workers, farmers, doctors, teachers, chefs, etc.) or help the head of the family to provide for their huge family (by doing paying jobs that builds something useful to be sold abroad or do paying jobs that think of ideas of how to provide more income and act upon those ideas).

The reason I envisioned a Socialist State to be a family is because it is a family. Ask the state for anything, and the head will strive to accommodate you just as how a father loves his children. As long as it does not cause problems towards others in the family and is of a reasonable request, we will strive our best for you.

The head of a household isn't just an entity to be honored and respected by the family but also it has its duty to the family, for the sake of stability, harmony, and the existence of the family for many generations to come.

The next topic that we have will talk about city building, a boring topic and a skippable one but is written for the sake of at least knowing basic knowledge about how early Socialists would end up building a city in our modern times.

VIII. The Execution Of Building Socialistic Cities

THIRD GRAND CHAPTER :
BUILDING SOCIALISTIC CITIES &
ITS ENVISIONED GUIDELINES

PREVIOUSLY WE DISCUSSED: what societies within Socialism will be like, what are the rules, what are the perks, what are the restrictions. But right now, I would like to give light to the plans of how those cities would most likely be built in this current time and age.

Because Socialism, as I have made the readers to understand, does not allow itself to be forced unto an existing society that already has an ideology because of the resistance that might appear. Therefore the best way is that Socialist societies will have to start by first finding usable land and building a city from scratch over that new piece of land. This will definitely not bother anyone and will have no such resistance. Once it is built, people will be gathered (with several conditions to be agreed upon first) to live within the walls of that city.

How can the city building process be done? Money & time are the two huge factors when it comes to city building. If we could use technology to our advantage it would be a big plus for both during and after the development process.

Without much further ado, I would like to give a basic structure of the city building process.

1. Land

THE MOST NEEDED thing when building cities or civilizations. Most lands are either privately owned or government-owned. But in this case of building a city, permission is needed and will be quite difficult to obtain because you want to build a city and call it your own city. Because every land is within the confines of a country, permission must be asked towards the country.

We will have to tell that government that we want a piece of land as big as Singapore to plan a city which will in the near future, help people from around the world get a job and a home and a life. We also intend on helping refugees, the poor, and people who are fed up with their own country and are finding for a better place to call home. The city will use an enclosed economic system where if there exists a currency, that currency will not be usable outside the walls of the city. And we will also have to say that the city itself will not be a part of the country hence will not follow the laws and values of the country's ideology but rather will be using a Socialistic Ideology to govern the lives of the people within the city.

If we are going to build a Socialist city within a democratic country, the permission will be quite difficult. But I believe a deal could be struck. One of the deals that I have in mind is this. We tell the government that we will give something to them in exchange for that piece of land and their aid in building and planning the city.

(I am not someone that is willing to give leverage to other parties over the city that I want to build for people. But if there is no other way to strike a deal that will in the future better the lives of people, then I'll have to do it and make sure we could end that leverage before I pass away.)

But what can we give in return for land, permission, and aid to build a city inside that country? What can we give that will not in the future bring instability to the city or bring difficulties to the people of the city? What we can do is, tell them that we'll sell our excess food or our excess generated green energy to the country at a lower price than the pricing we give other countries. Or we could think of something else but whatever it is should not allow our people to lose hope towards the governing body of our city.

But it would be best that we could buy the land from them and get permission without having to be indebted to them in any way. Maybe we could find a Socialist country that will allow us to build our city there or find some other better means as opposed to striking a deal that gives others leverage over us.

Suppose we get the land, what next?

2. Food Supply For The City

THE SOURCE OF human survival — water and food. We will need to hire professionals to plan out our water supply. As for our food supply, we will either need a full manual labor workforce or we buy automated technologies that will make farming easier. (But we still must need people who understand traditional farming just in case, in the long run, something goes wrong with technology.) With automated farmlands, we just need people to do more supervising than to do manual labor.

For food, we need livestock animals that will produce milk, eggs, and meat. We will have to purchase them from various places and transport them to our land. We will need farmlands for vegetables, fruits, spices, and others. We will need fishing boats for fish meat. This will imply that where we buy our land may need to be somewhere near waters where fish are present and also we must be permitted to fish, in order that the city will have fish on the menu. If we don't want fish or prawns or crabs or lobsters as our basic supply of food, that's okay too.

Because at the beginning of the building process we will not be able to do trade with other countries because there is nothing for us to sell in order for trade to commence, the inhabitants of the city will have to eat whatever the land provides without being grumpy about it. In fact, if the land can only grow rice, therefore it would be wise to tell the inhabitants of the land that there is only rice and for the long run it would be best that the inhabitants get used to rice because we do not want anarchy to appear just because of food preferences which is ridiculous and immature. If the land can only grow rice, the citizens will have to live with it. This is one of the drawbacks of an enclosed economic system and that is to force the people to be happy with what the land can provide. But in the future, if we, as the governing body, can provide better food choices to the inhabitants, it would be the duty of the state to do that good thing unto the people.

3. The First Inhabitants Of The City

I F THERE IS a 'First', there would be a 'Second', 'Third', and so on. Every country or city needs people to live and work within them. What sorts of people is Socialism trying to help? These are the exact people we are hoping to fill our cities with.

Socialism came about because of the atrocities that appear in the world. Our main goal is to help people who are suffering and currently living unbearable lives with poor living standards. People that don't know how to live, people who are giving up on life, people who are mistreated by their employers and by the cruelties of society, people who are poor or homeless, people with difficulties in earning sufficient money for the needs of their families. Also, the refugees, who are fleeing from their country because of wars, famine, drought, financial instabilities. These are the main people we would like to extend our hands to. In fact, these types of people are the only ones who will be hardworking enough to successfully bring about the success of the development process of the city.

If other countries do not want to take in refugees, then give the refugees to us and we will build homes and cities for them, and they will be our first inhabitants. If there are countries that are persecuting their own citizens, don't persecute them, rather allow them to come over, we will gladly accept them.

Why do I say that refugees are the potential could-be residents of Socialism? Because they are currently not living comfortable lives. People who are living comfortable lives will not want to enter into another society but it is those who are living uncomfortable lives that are willing to move in. Psychologically speaking, refugees are finding for a home, for a job, for a life, for sustainability, and if they can find it within another city regardless of the ideology, they will be willing to build and work in those cities.

Bottom line is that I would prefer the first residents of the city consists of people who have a desperate need to live whatever their background or status currently is. It is these people that will help build the city and be willing to assimilate into the laws and regulations of Socialist societies. After the city is built then it would be open to other people who are not currently desperate to live.

Coming back to the topic at hand. We have now come to having farmlands and livestock and boats. How can we get our first habitants to be willing to be farmers, tend to livestock, or be gathering fish from the sea when their previous occupation may not be in the manual labor sector? The easiest way is to ensure that we have sufficient money to purchase both the technology and the services of professionals, to build automatic farmlands so that most of the first inhabitants will not need to do much manual labor but learn to supervise the robots or technology that is used to do that work for us.

I do not want to imagine how it would be if we have to ask them all to perform manual labor for the first 2 to 5 years. But in the event where we who plan to build the city have limited funds, there is not much we could do than to tell them that they will have to do manual labor to get our city running in its early stages or even for the long run. But hopefully, there are sufficient funds to support automated farmlands, automated fish farms, and other automated usages for our drinking water and food supply.

What are the perks that a Socialist city, in its building process, can offer to the first inhabitants of the city or to the people who help build the city? We can promise them an additional layer of incentives that will be given to them **in the future**, for taking part in building the city, once we have laid out the local currency of the land and have started giving salary to members of society.

[Do not worry. The state or governing body in Socialism will (once the city has been developed) manage society in such a way that everyone will have a job and will be compensated for whichever job he (1) chooses to do or (2) is needed by the state to do. The compensation will be paid in local currency. The compensation will be split into different layers of wages. The first layer being a fixed basic income (similar to the workings of UBI) for all working citizens. This basic income will be sufficient for an individual adult to feed himself 3 above-average meals a day throughout the course of a month. In other words, this basic income fulfills his basic needs as a human being. The following additional layers of wage that every particular job will have will be based on the factors of the work being done (eg. the difficulty of the work, the out-reach of people it provides for, the popularity of the work, and various other factors). In total, the wage of a single working citizen will be more than enough for himself yet still be able to support his needs for entertainment, culinary indulgences, and other activities too.]

What will these people eat during the early stages? The first inhabitants will be divided into two groups of people. (1) The workers, and (2) the chefs & cooks of society. The chefs & cooks will have a place all across the farmlands and job areas where they receive food from storehouses to cook meals and bake bread for both the workers and themselves. In the early stages, people will both work without pay and eat the meals given to them.

What I like to think about is the type of food various people from different backgrounds and culture, that end up joining in building this city, could offer the whole society. Although the land can only generate food that is available in the land to grow, I strongly believe that various kinds of food or snacks or delicacies would keep the people entertained and happy throughout the city development process and also when the city has been developed, I hope to see other creative culinary that can be thought out to make happy the everyday lives of the people.

But if we do not have the luxury of technology, then the city building process will require manual labor for fish farming, crops (fruit, vegetables, spices) farming, animal farming, and others that are needed for both our food and water supply.

What I would like the reader to do (because without technology, we will have to do everything in a traditional way) is to imagine a simple society where we have firstly, the people who cultivate, farm, and collect our **raw** food supply, and secondly, the people who shall cook them. By having these two groups of people, we would have a simple working functional society where the workers of the field bring raw food to the chefs and the chefs in turn do their functional tasks of cooking the meals for the whole society. From these 2 groups working together, we could in the future add more different workers to upgrade civilization to consist of other jobs. (This is a simple way to see how a society can be formed from the ground up — through first just having farmers and chefs.)

Where will the first inhabitants sleep? Now the outline of the city will be that the city area will not be near farmlands and so quarters and simple housing will be accommodated for the workers and chefs to be built within the area of their workplace in the development stages of the city. This brings about the need for factories that produces building materials, and the availability of building architects and the construction workforce — another set of jobs that can be handed over to our first inhabitants. A medical workforce and education workforce would be a nice-to-have as well for society in the early stages.

Readers are probably wondering why not build the city first and then gather the people to become inhabitants. The reason we need to secure the food supply first and grow the food supply using a human workforce is because we are using an enclosed economic system that will be heavily dependent on what the land can produce. Also because the future power of trade from the city will be most likely through the export of food to other countries, people are required to have the knowledge to produce food. If the Socialist who wants to build the city, has the money, it would be easier to build the city and the farmlands at the same time and do all the other things in parallel but if he has limited funding, he will have to plan the city step by step from the food supply as a means to feed ourselves first. (Also before the first harvest is presented to us, we may need money to feed the people whilst waiting for crops and meat to be available.)

Having all these necessary jobs in the outskirts of the city area will be sufficient to bring about the existence of little village communities for the outskirts area where people who work there may not need to travel to the city area and back to the outskirts area on a daily basis.

What about the professionals that we hire? What are we going to pay them in exchange for their expertise and teaching insight? There are two ways to go about this. We could (1) ask them to be a part of our inhabitants where they will in the future be given an additional layer of incentives, or (2) we pay them, with money taken from our own pockets, throughout their temporary stay in the development process.

4. Electricty & Forms Of Energy

THE PREFERRED ENERGY generators would be green energy. Money will have to be used to purchase our source of electricity for both the different work areas and the city area. Being able to generate our own electricity will be a big plus because we could sell excess energy to other countries as a means of trade just as how we did the same with our excess food.

With green energy, this means that we could set up energy-harvesting even within the city and residential areas in addition to having an energy sector outside the city area. Out of the fear of sabotage or natural disasters that could hit one part of our land, we may need two to three external locations for our energy sector. (This could also be done for livestock and farmlands so as to ensure that if one of them is struck with a disease or something else, we don't end up losing everything because our eggs are not all in one basket but are in 3 different baskets. By doing it this way, we are also sure to be able to accumulate excess food and energy at any given time.)

There are many ways energy can be collected and stored, all we need to do is find the technologies and implement them, be it in the ocean or on land, be it through the use of wind, sunlight, the flow of water or gravity, there should be a cleaner way to get electricity that does not pollute our surroundings.

5. Construction Of City Area

THE MOST COMPLICATED process of all. We need to plan out the city and its future different sectors — the spacing of roads and pavements and the ventilation of the city area. Real professionals are needed for this job. But overall, it includes the detailed planning of waterways, drainage systems, waterworks, sewage systems, garbage dumps, telephone lines, electric grids, roads, houses, various buildings, etc. We may need a form of transportation between the residential area of the city to the outskirts of the city where the automated farmlands are. We need to know if we want underground transportation or trains on the surface and many other things within the city and where to place them. But what I am interested in is the residential housing, the places to eat, the stores to buy necessities of life and of the living, transportation and recreational area or areas where people can relax and find entertainment.

For housing, as a means to save space for other developments, I would prefer following the housing flats of Singapore. The flats in Singapore have mailboxes for each house situated in the lobby area. They are not of much use today but we could modify them to be useful for today's uses. Also, people could throw their garbage down big pipes without having to go out from their houses which is convenient. Drying the laundry is also doable from whichever floor your house is on.

As for places to buy food / products or seek for services (eg. laundry, barber, salon, massage, etc.) should be located near residential areas. But because we use an enclosed economic system, you won't be finding many varieties of things to buy, in fact, you may only see one brand wherever you go and that is the city-owned brand which implies that everything is produced within the land of the city and packaged also by the city. As you may already know, every job is given by the state to the people and so most of the products on shelves will be a state-owned product. We may start to see a variation of goods in shelves after we have done trade with other countries and receive their goods to be put on those shelves. That will be the future hope — to bring more varieties for selection towards the people. Aside from food products and mineral water, we may also need factories to produce: kitchenware, hygiene stuff (eg. soap, shampoo, toothbrush, scrub, etc.), at least basic clothing, medicines, and basic furniture (including beds). As for electronics and technology for individual uses (which were not present in the 1800s as a means of societal happiness), the inhabitants may have to wait a while before the state could provide their availability within the society.

(It may seem unfeasible that anyone would be willing to live like this for the next 5 years but give it some time and allow the minds of the state to work towards your desired favor.)

About transportation, every city planner has their own style in what should be used but for public transport. As known by the readers, people in these Socialist cities will not be having private-owned vehicles because of the various evil that could be done concerning those vehicles which may harm individuals or society as a whole, and so only government-owned transportation will be available for the public. For my preferences of public transport, magnetic trains and city bicycles would be nice. Green energy-powered scooters, buses, and cars may even be available.

Lastly, recreational areas. Parks, gardens, sports hall, bars, piano / live music lounges, etc. With time, these places could be provided. Recreational areas could also be made in a creative way to pave the way for tourists to spend money within our city and provide another source of income to the city.

Once we have our food supply, electricity generators, factories, and our city setup filled with residential areas, recreational areas, eateries, shops, and other buildings, we would have a society where every individual has a job and each is rewarded by the services of others. But to tackle future laziness and to make the system fairer, once the city has been developed, paper money will start to be issued and prices will start appearing in shops and food courts. The people who build the city have to be given this information and the wisdom thereof before they participate in the city building process to prevent a misunderstanding that may surface because of the change from **free** food and other things to **paid** food and other things.

Surely, there will emerge grumpy people within the early stages of city building because our land may not be able to produce certain kinds of food or vegetables whereas they are used to food we don't have, and grumpy people may also appear after the city has been built because we do not have high-end technologies or other forms of entertainment where they had them when they were in their home countries. These problems can be tackled through trade with other countries that have them. But the problem is, because the Socialist society uses an enclosed economic system (where our paper money has no value to the outside world), in order to do trade with other countries, we might need something that can be used for trade.

Food is one of the basic needs of mankind and is the most valuable item in trade therefore our Socialist societies, must have more farming grounds for food where we can use excess food from our side to trade with other countries. The economic theory is this. First, we need to be able to feed ourselves. And then we can use excess food to sell to other countries and the most interesting thing about selling food that we **do not need** is that we could sell them at crushingly low prices in such a way that countries are willing to buy our produce. And so we must produce more food than we can eat every month so that we can sell them to other countries. (Food does have an expiry date so there's no use in keeping them anyway.) And then with the money that we obtain from those countries, we buy either (1) the wants of the people or (2) the services that bring about the wants of the people. We could either buy the products of technology or for example ask the owner (directly) of KFC or IKEA to allow their idea to enter into our society and as payment, we do an agreement with the owner himself with regard to what our society could provide him / her and their family (or something else of that contract-based nature). And at the end of our business trip to the country, we release the paper money that has been obtained through the sales of our excess produce, back into their country by purchasing other things from that country.

Trade and economics is the most interesting part in the Socialist cities that I have envisioned that uses an enclosed economic system. This is because we can do trade without harming any country's economy. But the downside is that we end up getting grumpy people because we do not have free trade where the people can directly do business with other countries but every transaction or wants by the people must pass through the state and the state will do it on behalf of the people.

Aside from selling food, we can also sell other creative things that can be thought out by any individual who is also willing to share that idea with the state. Because everyone in society keeps everyone afloat, people do not have to work many hours and so have enough time for themselves to do all sorts of things.

The final city is a society where the state works for the people and provides their wants and needs and where the society itself does their respective jobs so that society itself can function properly. It is simple but may require huge amounts of money, available and usable land space, green energy generators, and the hiring of professionals for city building and its management. We need a lot of money to purchase the landmass, to buy and set up our energy-generation sector, to buy our first batch of livestock of various kinds, to buy seeds and farming equipment, to hire architects and other temporary professionals that will give us knowledge at the same time while working.

Because the city building depends on many factors, a clear action plan must be formulated. Where will factories be, how large is the city area, how many farmland sectors do we want as a measure of precaution from sabotage or natural disasters happening to one area. The list goes on. But once everything is done and paper money has been issued and prices have been released, then the final part is the setting up and making clear of the rules and regulations that will be found within the walls of the city with regard to the life of every individual within that city.

In what I have envisioned, just as a basic wage is given for any working individual, basic housing is given for free to the people with regard to their family size. The more children they have, the more the size of the basic housing, they will receive, is. Most of the rules and regulations have been talked about in previous chapters. The only thing I fear is that once the city is done, and children are begotten to the inhabitants of the city, when they grow up, the children may want to impose Democracy unto the Socialist society. This is a big NO from the system itself. If people in the future want to try Democracy, they could be sent off to democratic countries or we could ask them to do what we did and that is to build another city on another piece of land from scratch and create their own ideology there but do not disturb the current ideology in place within the society.

6. Final Notes About City Building

W E MUST REMEMBER the reason we want to build a society from scratch is to be able to ensure that people have jobs, people can live, and have a place to stay. We ensure that people are protected from the actions of their peers because the state regulates the activities and the jobs and the prices and how life is lived within the city. As long as the state understands its function to the people, the people need not fear. The early stages don't seem quite bright yet but as long as the state has a strong longing to please the people, wonders can be done; the inhabitants will just have to give it time.

The inhabitants will just have to be happy for what they currently have, which is, (1) not having to compete for a job, (2) not having to starve because of the hoarders of paper money, (3) do not need to be homeless because basic housing is given for free, (4) does not need to worry about education because it is also provided for you as long as you are willing to learn, (5) does not need to fear because your neighbor indirectly cares for you by being an employee of the state and working in society to ensure the continual existence of the society, (6) and have other securities.

The state is obligated to read your letters, the state is obligated to meet with you and know what you want and do all things to help you. Why does the state do this? Because it is required for the state to care first for the people **before we could hope** that the people be caring to one another. Because the goal of Socialism is to bring about a society that cares for society itself, therefore whatever you need, I, as the state will try my best to provide it for you so that in the event that I cease to exist, whatever your fellow human being needs, **you** will provide and hence bring about a continual mindset of love.

That is the ultimate end goal of Socialism — society will one day govern itself without the governing body (the state). On that day, a society will consist of every individual being a part of the governing body that governs itself because consciously, every individual has the same understanding and willingness to love their neighbor as themselves (causing each person to continue doing whatever job the society needs them to do). Therefore the state, while it exists, will build the mindset within the people by loving the people and caring for both the wants and the needs of the people.

The only reason Socialism is never achieved is because the end goal is a society that has no ruler or king over it **but yet** is able to function as an ever-existing society. And this can only be achieved if everyone in that society does not have self-interest but have a collective interest in the continual existence of the society itself. Every individual in society must conform to the same principles of life. Evil must be suppressed and be incapacitated of its motivation thereof. And the only way a human being can think of, that halts the motivations that may lead to evil, is by restricting the freedom of every individual in society. These restrictions restrict not good values but rather tend to restrict all the actions that may cause a future bad impact on society.

In religion, there exists a place called heaven where people who die but have good values within them will enter and those who do not have good values will enter into some other place. But like I said, as a human being who is **trying** to create a place without evil on the face of the earth where I, as that human being, cannot see who is good and who is bad, I along with other Socialists minds alike, have no other choice than to design a system which restricts everyone in the society for the sake of societal harmony.

IX. Christian Virtues Found Within Socialism

I JUST HAD to touch upon this topic because of what was found in the 'Final Notes About City Building', the previous text just before this one.

Christianity and Socialism are two different things. Even though I am a Christian, my Socialist view is not a Christian Socialist view. Maybe some of the readers may be wondering, why then does it sound like I am relating Socialism to that of Christianity?

I find it interesting that the ultimate goal of Socialism and the process to reach it as thought by wise early Socialists men are similar to the process by which Christianity teaches its members to conform to the goodness of the leader of Christianity (which is God), so as to bring about a society where every member consciously chooses to do good even though they understand how evil could be done.

Christianity teaches that only those who are capable of living good lives, striving to live good, and choosing good (also having the belief of the Son, Jesus Christ) will be given the keys to everlasting life. The mindset of Socialism is different. Socialism wants to bring about a form of goodness to the whole society, not because of the existence of Heaven and the requirements of Heaven, but because to achieve a form of continuous coexistence of societal harmony that will endure throughout the ages on the face of the earth, the human beings living on the face of the earth is required to understand goodness and with wisdom **choose** goodness over evil in order that society keeps on existing without breaking down due to an emergence of someone with self-interest.

In the case of Christianity, it is written that in Heaven, those who die and go to Heaven will be like the angels in Heaven, who do not marry and have children. Socialists understand that wisdom is not passable from the parent to the child. Wisdom is obtainable because we who live 'the life' understand 'the life' lived and obtained the experience and understanding to not make the same mistake again. But newborn children will always be curious as to why the laws made by the adults should be listened to word by word. In other words, while we live on the face of the earth and have children, with the existing good values of the parent (if the parent chooses good because of wisdom obtained through life), does not mean that the child born from that parent will automatically likewise choose to have the same values the moment he is able to speak and understand.

There is a study that says that an advanced species (if aliens exist or something of that nature) will choose to shut off their reproductive organs as they reach immortality, so as to prevent the next generation (which will start with 0 wisdom) from changing the laws that have been set in stone that prevents the future downfall of the species.

This brings the understanding whereby in the Christian religion, God sets up rules and laws for man to follow. Yet because of curious minds, some slowly transgressed those laws which have no visible impact on their generation or on their children's generation but have an impact on future generations.

If I may touch upon eating fats and the Christian religion as an example. We know that cholesterol, diabetes, and other similar things can be passed from the parent to the child in such a way that when a child eats a small amount of fat, it could trigger cholesterol if the parent has cholesterol. In the Christian world or rather the Jewish world as informed by the Bible, fats were not to be eaten by the priests of the temple neither were they to be eaten by the people. The fats of the animal when sacrificed to God, are to be burned to please God. No man should eat 'the fats', it was the law that the portions of fat belong to God. In other words, God protected the illnesses of the modern-day by making some things forbidden to be consumed in the past. But because the first man who curiously ate fats enjoyed it, although he probably didn't die from cholesterol, the effects are found today in our modern societies with their many complications. (With this I would like to highlight the following statement. By being in perfect obedience to God, who is wise, if mankind did obey God, mankind may not have stumbled upon disease. Therefore evil can be seen as opposing God, and when you oppose God who is wise, because of your disobedience, you will most likely end up in a messed-up state. I believe that the angels who know such a wisdom as this, blindly follow their wise God because that is the wisest thing to do — following whatever the wise one told them.)

We Socialists also have the same fear that even though we as human beings may obtain the wisdom not to do this and not to do that because it may cause something to happen in the future, it does not stop the next generation from crippling the laws we have set up for the continual existence of society. It is because of this that we Socialist have to be very restrictive towards the whole society because people can enter into our societies and change us from within or a child could be born tomorrow as a member of our society and sought to change our way of life that may be harmful to society in the **long run** although problems may not appear in the short run when the changes are made.

Therefore the problems of evil and self-interest, the motivations that give rise to bad moral choices and actions, from the Christian or religious standpoint are fought or are being tackled by giving or dictating good values towards the members of the religion. Whereas from the Socialist standpoint, we fight off these bad vibes of human nature and characteristics by restricting freedom which does indeed give off a sense of authoritarianism but is actually countering evil just the same as how Christianity counters evil by asking their congregation to have good values. So the bottom line is that there is a similarity between the goals of Christianity and other religious beliefs to rid the world of evil as is also the goals of Socialism.

A good wise Socialist leader wants the people to conform to the same values, understandings, and principles that he has, in which he believes is the ultimate lifestyle for the goal of an everlasting society on the earth and so he, as a human being, does all that he can to bring about that end result.

In the same way, Christianity wants the people to conform to the same values, understandings, and principles of the Creator, which is without a doubt more knowledgeable and wise than any human being (or any Socialist), and this is done to achieve a people who one day will be able to live and coexist with God who resides in Heaven. For God who is holy and righteous is not willing to coexist with those who are wicked and evil but only those who are pure at heart and share the same values as God. And when they have the same mindset as God, they and God will be **One**. (**'One'** does not mean 'one and the same'. But 'One' means having the same way of thinking which means to say that those who have the same way of thinking will cause them to agree on everything and coexistence is possible only at that point in time — where man coexists with God because he is in agreement with God concerning all things.)

As a last note, Christianity allows free will because God wants to prepare for himself a people who out of their own free will, chooses goodness over intentions of evil, chooses values of coexistence rather than values of self-interest. Why? Because God himself has free will and chooses to be Holy and Righteous over evil and wicked. Therefore God wants his people to be like Him in order for them to live happily ever after together.

Socialism on the other hand, because it was created by a human being, the mindset thereof found within Socialism is a logical mindset of how to bring about a harmonious society that will always exist and flourish on the face of the earth, where Evil is always present in the hearts of man and may at any point in time suddenly spring into action that causes societal disruptions and breakdowns. It is because of our understanding as Socialists that evil will forever be present on the earth that the only way to have an everlasting society, is to eliminate freedom **but** we must also ensure that the people within society understand the wisdom behind **the reasoning why freedom is to be restrained**. This is an important point that must be understood by every generation that is found within the Socialist cities so that the city will forever be governed by the Wisdom to not deviate from the (already) working, functioning laws of society.

SECTION E

INFORMATION CONCERNING THE AUTHOR, COMMENTARIES & HIS LAST WORDS

Preferring Socialism Over Democracy : Envisioning Cities Of Societal Harmony & Continual Coexistence

I. The Socialism Of This Man (A Writing From The Year 2017)

Information Concerning The Author, Commentaries & His Last Words

T HE CHILDREN OF today are intelligent people — those who are in primary school as of the year, 2017.

I was born in the year 1990. Only a few of the people at that time were intelligent. Some of that few may have bright futures today. But will the intelligent children of today, be the society builders of tomorrow?

The definition of builders here is not to be seen as businessmen or successful professionals in life. Rather builders here means, those who help contribute to society, those who are in the government, or even the President himself. Will our children become the people who will push our country forward, bring stability to the life of citizens or rethink the strategies for our country's economy?

We see today very few numbers of young men who strive for their country's well-being. In fact, probably very few my age have put aside some time to think about the economy, to think about how to get people to follow pedestrian rules, or even what could be done to ensure happiness for all.

Now, the spark towards having my current ideology started out during the second quarter of 2008. At that time I chose to quit the school I was attending and try to get into a Polytechnic in Singapore. My goal in life at that time was to become an Aerospace Engineer which seemed to me as the highest paying job in the world. The reason I wanted a high-paying job was because back when I was fourteen, I wanted to later in life marry the girl I love and open up an orphanage. And to sustain the life of the children in the orphanage, I would need the highest paying job I could think of, which led me to aerospace engineering.

I went to Singapore in early April. I searched for the Polytechnic that had Aerospace Engineering and I tried to enroll. A woman told me that the class wasn't available (probably having seen that I got an E for the Cambridge English Examination) and that they would inform me. In the end, I went back to Indonesia and waited a year. At the end of my wait, nothing happened. They didn't inform me about anything at all.

During that year in which I had nothing to do, I spent most of my time surfing the internet. I went from reading comic books online to downloading Japanese animated cartoons. After three to four months I find myself reading articles. One article led to the next and before I knew it, I was reading about the economy. At home, I started writing down notes. I tried to figure out how the economy works. I searched online about paper money which eventually led me to understand why inflation had to take place.

To me, the thing which bothered me at that time was this. (I am a Christian and so I have this belief in the existence of a God.) God created men to live on the earth and to rule over it. As long as men toil the ground, no one will die of hunger. Only those who are lazy to toil the ground will have nothing to eat unless they have something of value to trade in exchange for food with those who do toil the ground. That was a time of barter. At that time I didn't see barter as a bad thing but I kept on hearing people saying to me that barter was a complicated system to use. This statement is a debatable one. The only thinking that I allow myself to understand from their statements was that barter uses or ends up as an inconsistent trading system. It wasn't complicated, it was just inconsistent. Because I sell 1 Kg of rice for 2 buckets of milk today and the next day you come to me asking for rice, I can ask you for 3 buckets of milk in exchange for 1 Kg of rice, and the following day I can ask for something else with regard to whatever my heart wants. But this in itself is not even a problem. It doesn't even count as a problem if it is compared to inflation, which is the big problem in our every economy.

The economy of the world shifted from barter to coins issued by governments. From there we shifted towards paper money issued by banks.

Thinking about the economy was what sparked the ideology that I currently have. The economy isn't just a facet of living. It isn't something to be taken lightly by any government. Every single person depends on the economy of their country. We do not depend on technology, we depend on the economy. If the economy is bad, even a civilized nation may turn into a barbarous one. In other words, the economy plays a big part in every individual's life.

Aside from the economy of the country which is thought of by every government, there exists also the economy of the individual. Both these economies are two separate things. A country's good economy doesn't actually make sure that every individual is living, financially, healthy lives. Likewise, if every individual has a good economy, it doesn't mean that the country is having a good economy. Very few governments around the world actually care for the economy of every individual mostly because it isn't possible to do both and for them, they would rather choose the economy of the country because statistically speaking, if the economy of the country is good, therefore on average, people (or the majority thereof) should be living good lives.

Because we are talking about 'statistically speaking', so the worst-case scenario of a country known to have a good economy could be a country where only 40% of its citizen are living above average whereas the other 60% are living below average.

Back in 2008, I asked myself this question how is it possible that a country known to have a good economy, has about 30% to 60% living below average. The only possibility of this happening is to imply that there are people who hoard paper money. They may not hoard paper money intentionally but due to their booming business(es), they end up with, money, enough to raise a thousand children into adults.

Paper money is to be used as a medium of exchange, to be used during a transaction of trade, from one person to the other, & not to be kept in banks. The people must understand that only so much paper money is printed out meaning that there is a limit to the amount of paper money printed out. And for others to have that medium of exchange, one has to use his medium of exchange, in order that the others can also be able to do trade using paper money. Paper money was made to go around, not to be kept. Hence the ideal usage of paper money is to have everyone spend what they earn over a period of one month as long as they have an occupation or business and if one has excess paper money, he should trade that paper money for gold or land or house or wooden furniture or wine and keep those instead of keeping paper money which was created to be used as a medium of exchange. This is the ideal usage of paper money. I am not asking anyone to do this, because I myself do not do this. The reason is probably a universal one — we want to store money for future uses, which isn't wrong. But the system we use doesn't allow us to store it if we want a country with no poverty. I am just saying that this is the ideal usage of paper money and let me emphasize once again, to be used as a medium of exchange and not to be kept or stored. And because it (**paper money**) is to be seen **not as wealth** but as **a medium used to exchange for things**, the **ideal way** is to **use it**.

[We all have the right to keep wealth (eg. gold, house, car, etc), we do not need to give away our wealth. But paper money is different, dear ladies and gentlemen. It can never be seen as wealth because it is needed by the society. The people that invented paper money, where one of its characteristics is **being limited in number**, intended for paper money to be seen not as wealth (not as something you can keep) but as something that the society (people) can use so that life for every single human being in society can continue to exist (to eat & to live). I believe not many people in 2021 (the year this paragraph was written on), even know this fact. Most hoarders of paper money do not know this and I believe governments too are unaware of this because if they are aware of what paper money was created for, they should be reminding their people what paper money is once every 10 years or so.]

If I have a set of great wooden furniture made from China. That's all I have left. I am broke and I am jobless. I need the medium of exchange to do trade for bread and so I have to sell that furniture that has been in my family for twenty years that has a current value of 4 years of employment worth of paper money but none of the hoarders of paper money (the supposedly rich in the understanding of the world) wants to buy the furniture. I can't even get a month's worth of salary for it. In the end, I died because I couldn't buy food. And in order to buy food, I have to get that medium of exchange but no one wants to give it to me in trade for my wooden furniture. This story emphasizes the need for paper money to go around because people need to use it in order to live, in order to eat, in order to do trade.

I sound like someone who is dictating the readers to implement the ideal usage of paper money in their daily lives. But that's not what I am trying to do. During the first half of 2009, I said to myself if ever I become president, one of the things I would address first, is to give the people an understanding of what paper money is — a medium of exchange, and what actually happens when inflation does happen. After that, I will talk about the ideal usage of paper money in the hopes of frightening those who keep paper money into buying land or gold or something so that the medium of exchange does end up flowing to another person. And in that same speech, I will add two other points. First, that I would raise the taxes of the people who have a huge sum of paper money in their bank accounts. Second, I will give them who have a huge sum of paper money, an option to invest in start-ups or to open up businesses that could help reduce the unemployment rate and at the same time end up having the medium of exchange that they carry to flow to their employees as wages. Those who do coordinate with the government to do these things, will not be made to pay the extra taxes that I mentioned as the first point. If the hoarders of paper money, under the worst-case scenario, a year after the speech, still is a threat to the economy of the individuals, then for the sake of the individuals, I would do inflation upon the economy that risks the probability of hyperinflation.

Inflation normally hits everyone. The rich, the poor, everyone gets hit. But at that time, I had thought of a way to make the inflation that risks hyperinflation, not hit the poor but only those who are rich in paper money. In theory, under strategically inflating the currency every month, and at the same time equally distributing the printed paper money into the bank accounts of the citizens starting with those who are known to be 'poor' in paper money, we should be able to distribute the value of paper money held by the 'rich', prior to the inflation process, to the 'poor', after or during the inflation process, in a legal manner. In simpler terms, it is the distribution of known 'wealth' as to the value of paper money prior to inflation, from the 'rich', and distribute it to the 'poor', through inflating the economy and equally distributing the printed money to the citizens. It is illegal for a government to forcefully take the money owned by the rich and give it to the poor. But it is very legal to distribute money from the rich to the poor through this inflation method. If the hoarders of paper money are a threat to the economy of the individual, this is what I was thinking of doing back in 2009 if I ever become president.

In October of 2017, there was a statement that I heard, talking about the ideal way of the economy of every country to ensure happiness for all countries. The way was simple but the ability of having it done that way is nearly impossible. The statement goes something like this, "To ensure good economies in countries, every country must have its exports and imports balanced. This way, countries will move forward together." I believe in this statement but it is not possible to have every countries' exports and imports balanced at the same time. We are not robots. In a world where vehicles are automated by Artificial Intelligence, there will be no such thing as a traffic accident. Robots are highly structured and systematic. Give them a set of rules and they will obey it for life. But humans aren't like that and so it isn't possible to have all countries' exports and imports balanced at any particular time.

As we progress forward, we are seeing artificial intelligence in progress. Soon we will have more automated farmlands where farmers are no longer needed. With the increase in technology, more or less in 40 years' time, jobs are going to be taken from us. There will be lesser jobs requiring a human workforce. This is only a good thing if the government owns every business there is in the country. Because the worst-case scenario for a country where business owners and factories have gone over to using automated machinery to do their work rather than inquiring a human workforce, 40% to 60% of the people will be permanently unemployed. If this happens during a time where we are using the current economic system, the economy of the individual will be in a hurting state. Corporations will be receiving more of the medium of exchange without handing it over to their employees because they do not own any human employees to give the medium of exchange to.

In the world today, there are some governments out there who give wages to those who are jobless. And these jobless people receive a fixed sum every month. If we are moving forward to the age of having an automated workforce replace a human workforce, to prevent the economy of the individual from ending up in a hurting state, we have to ensure that the government owns everything — implying that the automated robots will be working for us — those who will be jobless yet still be able to receive a monthly income issued by the government, and not implying that the robots be working for a group of people or individuals — which would end up hoarding the medium of exchange. This here can be seen as Socialism because the government owns everything, but my methods are not through force or revolutions.

Humans are curious, they are greedy, they are self-centered. This is the norm of a human being. The reader may be different, the writer may be different. I am just stating what is normal of a human being. If we allow humans to live their lives without supervision, people tend to hoard paper money for themselves. People tend to get more power for themselves as though life is a game for supremacy. Life should be a world of social interactions, sharing, quality time with people, and societal building. If the government does not open its eyes and see human beings as to how they themselves would like to be treated , then, we are on the verge of a future breakdown.

Then again, I am just talking about the worst-case scenario. Let's get back to the main topic of how I ended up seeing myself as a Socialist.

Back in 2008 / 2009, while I was understanding what is behind paper money, I found out that in order for me to set up a new country and issue a currency to that country, I have to borrow money from the world bank. I couldn't mine gold and base the issuing of printed paper money on the gold that was mined. There was no other way than to borrow money from the world bank in order to print the currency that will be used in the new country. Every country that is in debt with a bank, is indirectly known to be owned by that bank until the country is debt-free. The country may not be wholly owned by the bank but the bank has leverage over the country and this is a bad thing if the owner of the bank is a bad person. When a bad person has leverage over you, you are finished.

At that point in time, I learned that paper money was no longer backed by gold or silver or any kind of metal. I wasn't an economics student. I had to find answers to understand the shifts of our economy.

Because I had waited for a year and nothing happened, my parents were worried and I was put into an institution where I ended up with an associate's degree in Computer Science. I entered in 2009 and finished in early 2013 and I started working later that year.

I was raised in Singapore from the age of 2 years old to 12 years old. Therefore I was very obedient to traffic lights, pedestrian crossings, always keeping to the left side of the road. I knew what a queue is. I knew not to talk when someone else is talking. I am very disciplined with regard to laws that harmonize society. But the society in the capital city of Indonesia, Jakarta, wasn't very obedient to the social law. People were living as though they are alone in the world, as though no one is there other than themselves.

The people were self-centered at that time. Because of that, I ended up writing up a couple of programs that could give self-awareness to the people, of the lives of others that are living around them. I had a different speech I would like to do for the building up of character, of the Indonesian people, in conclusion telling them that laws were created not so that citizens will live in cages and government officials could roam around freely but rather laws were created so that we may respect the existence of our fellow countrymen in our daily lives and so harmonizes the country.

Coming to the end of 2010, I had several programs that I have written down to be implemented in Indonesia if I ever became president. I had plans to effectively decrease air pollution and at the same time make sure that both pedestrians, as well as drivers, understand the rules of the road. Included in this program was to see if the country could legalize public transport (most of which had some form of private ownership) and turn them into government-owned public transport. This was thought of to ensure public safety. In my mind was a thought that if the government could own public transports all over Indonesia, middle-class people and above may start trusting the safety of the then government-owned public transport.

Another program in which I had high hopes for was to re-evaluate rules, laws along with the punishment for breaking them. These included traffic laws, pedestrian rules, criminal offenses, corruption, petty crimes, email & SMS scams, punishment for dishonesty or lying usually done by bank corporations, insurance companies, and housing agencies towards citizens like not disclosing information that citizens should know of. A good salesman to me is someone who tells the side-effects of the products he is selling first before going into the good stuff. Tricking people into agreeing or signing contracts may not be a violation of the law. But if the possibility of these people ending up in deaths, with troubled peoples or hurting the economy of their own household which is the case for all of these tricks done by big corporations, then this becomes a government issue. When lives are being endangered, no longer is it just a matter between a business corporation and a single person; It becomes a government issue (or it should at least from my point of view have some form of government involvement).

These revised rules and laws will be posted online and in schools so that citizens could understand the rules and laws that have been placed over them. Within this program are other things that I wanted as well. I wanted to review the people currently behind bars and make sure that their punishment makes sense. I wanted to ensure good prison conditions. I wanted to make sure that if a man is charged 5 years behind bars and during the 5 years he loses an arm, I want the government to compensate him for his arm loss. Likewise, if a judge accidentally judges wrongly and sends a person into prison, I want to make sure he gets compensated for wasting time in prison for something he didn't do. I wanted the families who have lost children who were beaten to death under police custody or whilst being behind bars to be compensated for their losses. I want citizens to acknowledge that every human life is of value (and that citizens should not try to harm the economy or the condition of any of their fellow citizens).

Other programs include unemployment, programs to ensure the tricking of citizens done by corporations does not happen, programs of compensation from the government to citizens & taxes. I'd like to talk about taxes. Taxes should only be done one time for every single person. Whatever he buys with his remaining money after paying the tax for his wage, is being bought by money already being taxed. There are two options. We can do it this way or there is no tax for wages but everything the person buys will have tax cuts from that purchased item. Again, these were my thoughts in 2010 (when I was just 20 years old).

What I didn't thought about then in which I should add to my list of programs was a program for wages — to set up an ideal wage system in which companies must pay their employees who do own a degree or certificate. Currently, Indonesia does have a minimum wage amount that companies must give towards their employees but companies seem to wage those who do have a degree and those who don't, the same amount of money. To me this is wrong. Can you believe that there exist companies that pay Bachelor's degree students or even Double degree students below the standard? It is a miracle these graduates didn't end up killing their bosses for treating them like garbage by giving them low wages. This is a despicable act. Even to graduates with diploma certificates or to those having only high school qualifications, it isn't nice to pay them that low. But anyone who kills for any reason is subjected to judgment for it is not in the law to allow a man under any circumstance to take another man's life. It is the duty of the government to pursue an issue and it is restricted by law for a man to take an issue, regarding the life of another, into his own hands. Therefore it is highly demanded of the government to allow citizens to send letters regarding what they think is wrong with society and the government must read those letters because that is how citizens should be served, especially in democratic societies where the leaders are elected to serve the people.

[I personally feel like the governments in Democratic societies are serving the people but are lacking love and attention towards the livelihoods of the individuals. And so there is an unseen form of ignorance from the government due to the ideals of Democracy that doesn't allow the government to enter into the lives of individuals.]

There were two programs that I was revising, coming to the end of 2010. A program for idleness and a class nobility system program for citizens, where the higher you are in that class system, the more comfortable and simple, life will be for you in that country. Let me elaborate on both these systems. Of course, funding is always a big issue when it comes to accommodating the needs of government programs but allow me to show you the big picture of these two programs in which I find myself at the end of their writing down, fascinated by them and what they can achieve.

Now, the program for idleness is originally thought of for citizens 12 years old and above who had a lot of spare time and maybe nothing much to do. These also included youngsters who have dropped out of school because they cannot afford it, as well as adults who are uneducated, and / or jobless. Idleness is a big issue in society. Idleness can lead a person to do all sorts of things which most of the time tend to have a negative impact on one's life. In the world of religion, idleness is an invitation to the devil or evil spirits. And so idleness may not sound harmful but is an unconsciously big problem for society. Idleness is a sibling of boredom and maybe friendlessness.

The idleness program expanded at the end of the writing down of it, into a gigantic program that may sound quite fictionally difficult to see come into fruition. But for the sake of simplicity, let me just highlight the aspect of the program that will contribute to society.

In order to pull in people to want to follow the program, we have to use human psychology. What does a person, child or man, want in return for participating in a government program for its citizens? There was a couple of things that were thought out to draw people in. First of all, I was assuming that governments don't have enough funding to hire people to do social work. Therefore to lessen the funding burden, we use these idle people to do social work. They are supervised and get points for the work that they do. And then, the small funding the government has to hire social workers will be used instead to pay teachers for classes and courses that are 'job related' — the understanding needed for simple job employments, 'language related' — learning all sorts of languages, 'study related' — school stuff & study groups with supervising teachers, 'recreational activities related' — sports classes (swimming, badminton, ballroom dancing, self-defense, boxing, etc.). Now, the points that are obtained by the participants of this program will be able to be used to book these various classes that the government pays teachers to teach. Once a numbered threshold is reached, the class opens for them.

Because I was able to see a much better improvement for the program, I expanded it, adding to it phase 2 & phase 3 and the other following phases that come after that. In the end, it was a program for the whole country to indulge in, mostly young adults probably. You can find friends in the program. You can become part of a community in the program. At the end of the writing down of the program, I named the program "Indonesia's Color Brigade". It utilizes a militarized ranking system. It had senior and junior officers. It had layers of student council bodies. For government paying courses, there were added engineering courses, mechanic courses. People who had earned points can use the points to study engineering, become mechanics, doctors, bodyguards & militarized personnel. Higher-ranking officers can have more facilities and cheaper classes or courses. Points and tests are required for promotion. All these improvements were thought out as a means to pull people into the program and away from being idle. I may have gone a little too far by implementing a militarized ranking system but if this is needed to get youngsters and adults away from drugs and the negative stuff in life, then this is a good thing, I have not derailed from the original purpose of the program. But of course, we could just stop after phase one.

The second program was a class nobility system. I used human psychology as well for this one. How do you make sure people understand the rules and laws of this country and hope that they would implement that knowledge in their daily lives? It is similar to the previous program. If you give something in return, they might just obey the rules and regulations of societal living.

The class nobility system serves as a dual program. The first part of the program was to allow a randomly selected fixed number of people to enter the program once every one or two months. First, they have to learn basic rules. If they pass the test, they go up a rank in the nobility chain of class ranks. In every rank, they are given knowledge about rules and laws that the government imposed on its people to understand. Passing tests they go up ranks. Hopefully, their ranks can be stored in a government database that is linked to their citizen identification number. Certain ranks will have upgrades (example: lesser tax fees, lesser transportation fares, discounts at outlets that are working together with the government for the sake of society) to bring about a better life as a citizen. There is one disadvantage for the citizen. If the citizen is caught by the police doing a particular offense that he or she already passed the test for, it will be a very big problem for the citizen. His or her rank status will be non-active for a period of time and the punishment will be multiplied by a certain number.

The second part of the program is this. After they have reached a particular class rank, they are able to discuss programs with government officials. They will be capable of interacting directly with government officials. Going higher within the nobility ranks, citizens would be able to write their own programs and submit them to the government for approval. The bottom line is the higher members of the nobility system will be given the privilege to build society upwards together with government officials. So in other words, citizens don't have to be elected to be able to be government officials. But through this program, citizens may become like unto government officials working part-time.

By mid-2011, I had many things planned out. Although I started by thinking about the economy and ended up with various programs fitted for presidency, I was stuck with 2 things in mind. I had a thought that if I did ended up as a president, I would not be a president for the country but rather a social worker for the people. There is a difference between a president and a social worker for the people. That was the first thought that bothered me. The second thing was that I kept on thinking about the economy of the people, how do I implement the economic system that I had envisioned. Because I really didn't care for the economy of the country; I cared for the individual and to them, nothing matters more than the economy.

The economic system that I have in my mind today is the same economic system back then. The system to use an enclosed economic system and start a sub-country from scratch was already in my head at that time. It wasn't that the other programs didn't matter. To me, having the enclosed economic system implemented in Indonesia was all that I could think about. If this system cannot be brought into fruition, then under a future disaster, I don't know if we could survive it.

The creation of this sub-country not only helps individuals currently suffering from economic issues of their households, but under a crisis, a full-grown sub-country can help the main country. In conclusion, there are two advantages for the main country. The first is that the sub-country will take citizens from the main country. Let me use an example. Paper money medium amounting to trillions of rupiahs, used amongst 380 million people is lighter of a burden than to be used amongst 400 million people. This isn't an instant take out of 20 million people. Because the sub-country will be done from scratch, with due process and time, we may get to that number. It may take 10+ years to reallocate 20 million people from all over the country to a different location though. The second advantage is with full-grown sub-country, using an enclosed economic system, it can help the main country which is using the globally connected economic system through trade. And during a global crisis, that will not affect the sub-country, the sub-country would be able to lessen the economic impact that crisis will have upon the main country.

And so after my mind was filled with thoughts of urgency for the realization of my economic agenda, I said to myself that I needed the funds to do this because I was certain I would not be able to participate in a presidential election because firstly I was just 21 years old at that time whereas I need to be 35 years old to participate in it.

Secondly, I don't have any connection with any government officials to form a party. And thirdly, even if I do get a party, I am afraid of the people who will form a party with me because being in government is the easiest way to become a rich man. The temptations are present once you are in the seat of power. All you got to do is probably waste some saliva and you will be able to do corruption. My goal is for the people but I don't know if I could find people who are just like me in that sense to fill my party.

My goal from then was to get funds on my own also because my economic agenda may go beyond 10 years which is 2 terms of government in Indonesia. And to rely on government funding would be difficult because there will be many programs in the government that need funding before, during, and even after I served 1 or 2 terms. That is also if I do make it into the seat of presidency. Whereas I had the urge to get this economic agenda of mine going whether or not I do become president. Because as I have said, the financial happiness of the people which would end up harmonizing society, means a lot to me, both for the sake of this generation and the generations to come.

Now after knowing about me, you should be able to notice that my programs and economic agenda all had one thing in common and that is that they were all similar to that of programs and systems thought out of by Socialists.

Here is a list of things Socialists can be seen as through the programs I have given above, in this chapter.

Socialists hate bosses in a metaphoric sense because they normally work and gain very much more money than they give their employees whereas their spending is very likely the same as their employees which makes them single persons who have a lot of excess cash in hand. In other words, socialists hate inequalities. And so the economic goal of socialists is to have the people work for the people, not work for bosses or for people who seek tremendous wealth. And if a person's wealth can be used to aid other people whereas there are those who hoard up paper money (which has a limit to its numbers) for themselves, then it is best to not have them in society. As I have said in the early part of this chapter, you can keep gold but not paper money unless the paper money can be printed an unlimited number of times without causing inflation.

That is how I ended up seeing myself as one (meaning as a Socialist).

Now, I have stated that socialists hate bosses and likewise vice-versa, we are hated by rich groups of people. In socialism, we try to take people out of the world system where no one can affect us, where we can live in harmony away from global economic tides and waves. But what do rich people want? They want more wealth. And after obtaining more wealth they end up wanting power and control. And when they discover that they won't be able to control people living in socialism if they allow us to prosper in it, they do something about it. They do all this for the sake of their own selfishness and greed.

Another way to see it is this. If we rely on other people or countries to live our lives, we become vulnerable meaning we live under the influence of others which makes us controllable. But if we rely on ourselves to live, we don't need to worry about what other people or country is doing, they won't be able to affect our living in any way. This is what I meant by separating oneself from the global system which is done by using an enclosed economic system.

My Socialism concept is quite different from how the world sees Socialism. Phase two of Socialism isn't going to be Communism for me. I envision a Socialism that feeds and tends to the people within it, all the while using an enclosed economic system, can still do trade with those who use the open economic system to provide the people with things or technology that we currently do not have.

My hope concerning the use of this Socialist concept is so that it could not only be implemented in Indonesia but also in countries around the world, allowing every country to have a sub-country where all the people in those respective countries who are unable to live with a currency which is inflatable, will reallocate themselves into their country's sub-country where is located a socialist living environment for them to live in harmony and financial security.

Once again, I say this. I am not wanting to change the whole country to undergo socialism. I want to create a sub-country inside the country from scratch and allow that sub-country to undergo socialism for the sake of individuals who are having a hard time living under an inflatable economy. I don't even want to be president if I don't have to. All I want is to build the sub-country and make sure that the living needs of the people are capable of being taken care of. Life always comes down to economic issues. If we are living economically well, our lives become a blast.

[May the reader understand that more than 90% of this topic whereby talks about 'the Socialism of this man' was written in 2017.]

II. My Writings In 2018 : Refugee Crisis & The Semi-Restrictive Model

Information Concerning The Author, Commentaries & His Last Words

---

[THE FOLLOWING PARAGRAPHS are written in 2018. I find some of the things written here to be mind-opening and quite somewhat useful to understanding myself. What the reader will find here is a trying on my part to bring about the possibilities of having countries themselves help their fellow citizens or refugees that need a better form of living. As you know, my Socialist dream is to set up a city (without depending on investors) for people to live outside of the world but in the following written texts, I try to be realistic in my efforts and use existing countries to help their fellow human beings around the world. Take a read on the following that also includes my other writings within it. The following text is also supposedly the second last chapter of an unpublished book that I didn't finish back in 2018. As the reader reads this, there could be some parts that are interesting and others that are contradictory to what I have written prior to 'Information Concerning The Writer & Last Words', but I allow it to be present for some other reasons. Readers can choose to skip this whole chapter if they want to or to read this chapter separately on a different day.]

THERE HAVE BEEN a few countries that accommodate the stay of refugees in their countries. Refugees need safety, they need shelter, they need jobs. It is great for the countries who could extend their hand and cope with the people they bring in — give them proper jobs and be able to accommodate all those people at the same time. But for the countries which dare not look the other way but find themselves having a hard time coping with the numbers that they have extended their hand to, there is a way out from the hardships facing both parties.

People who live inside cities and countries that do not have any crisis, live not for shelter nor for food, because they already have that. They live for lifestyle, they live for an upgrade in their living standards. But the people fleeing their country of origin, will in the future want an upgrade in their living standards, but currently are in need of a place that could provide them with a long term stability, shelter, and jobs to feed themselves.

And so we set up for them a place that could give them just that for the time being. For the next 5 to 10 years, there is a way that every country could give them: a new place to live their lives, jobs that pay well. All these can be given to the refugees, with a minimum burden on the people of the country that extended its hand to these refugees.

There are thousands of refugees, that are around due to economic crisis, war crisis, and instability crisis. Aside from these, there are also people who are facing difficulties living and providing for themselves and for their families, even while living inside a country not facing a crisis. And so there are 2 groups of people needing the aid that we could give them, (1) refugees who flee their countries because of a crisis, (2) people who are having difficulties living in developing countries and even in already developed countries — probably because whatever job they take, wages them very low.

What then is the solution? I am a selfish person to the extent that I want to be the one who oversees the idea to its fruition and be the one who ensures the happiness of every individual myself instead of having someone else do it for me. But for the sake of a quick and swift solution to the world's problem, I am willing to share it with you. But before I could say it, I need you to understand that you have to listen to the details. You have to be attentive, you have to keep an open mind. Because if you read it quickly, what you will receive is an idea that will be seen as a pipe dream — something that is not possible, as something that defies the logic that the world has taught you to understand. And so I need you to have an open mind and read the following carefully so that you may receive the solution I am trying to convey to you.

What I am sharing with you is something big and I do not know where to start. There are many parts to the solution and you have to read all the parts to see the picture. In other words, it can only be understood as a whole, not in part.

What I am implying is to build a city from scratch and the early occupants of this city are those that currently in life, are looking for a stable life and jobs that could sustain a stable life — meaning that these people are in a dire need to live, to feed themselves, to have a permanent roof above their heads. These are the people that can and will be able to build a city from scratch. This city, once built, 5 to 10 years from the time of its building, will be a home for these people themselves and others like them that need what they originally need. All these could be done without burdening the countries that provide the land space, that will be given to the refugees or the people in need of stable living, to build upon.

The type of economic system used in the city, that will be built by the hands of the refugees and those who are a part of the second group of people who are in a dire need to live, is an enclosed economic system. My definition of an enclosed economic system is a system where the use of money printed by the city is only usable inside the city of origin. This means to say that the money used to give wages to them means nothing on the outside — it can't be used to purchase anything outside the city. Hence the people living in the city will not be able to do trade directly with people in other cities or countries.

Why should a country help build this city or other future cities that are based on an enclosed economic system? You will be helping two groups of people. (1) those who are in need of a better living condition — this could be refugees and/or your fellow countrymen who are struggling to cope with life's expenses, given the wages they receive, (2) in the event of an economic crisis, the countries who use an open economic system will have food prices rising but those who use my so-called enclosed economic system, will not be affected and so these cities you help build can help ease a part of the crisis your country will be facing. Aside from these, there are also a couple of economic problems that can be relieved by placing your countrymen who really need a better place, into an enclosed economic system. One of those reliefs is in the fact that reducing the population of people in a country where inflation affects the people, will allow wealth or paper money to circulate more easily. I say this because in theory, two countries in which one of them has twice the population as the other, but both having the same amount of wealth; the country that has the lesser population, under an equal distribution of wealth policy, will cause an individual to own more than the individual that lives in a country with more population. In theory, this is the study.

But in practice, this is not the case because a businessman, which is 1 person, owns a business and his business expands, owning many shops around the world. This, one man, becomes richer and richer. But it is not his fault that disables equal distribution of wealth. It is in fact the system that we use in the world that causes this unfairness. So it is not the man's fault for having a business boom and being rich. This man is just one of those lucky ones. And so with this understanding, this is just one of the reasons why my ideology has to use a restrictive system as we will see in the following paragraph.

There are two models that I have come up with that induce the use of a closed economic system. (1) a closed economic system that is partially restrictive of its citizens, (2) a closed economic system that is fully restrictive towards its citizens. I am more inclined to use the second model because with the second model I can ensure the prosperity of every individual and their descendants in the long run. But I am sure that people may prefer the first model because it allows the ownership of houses and businesses (to an extent), whereas it isn't allowed at all, in the second model.

If you read until this part and feel something is amiss, don't give up hope because there are wonders within the following paragraphs below. What you must know is that a good system cannot guarantee you all of the good things, there is no such thing as a perfect ideal system that allows freedom, security, safety, food supply, harmony, non-violence, anti-thefts (anti-crime), etc. Democracy gives the people freedom but there are some crucial things in the list that are crossed out. Democracy does not mean that criminals do not go about their businesses. Democracy does not ensure that everyone is waged above the standard given by the government. What I am saying is that every ideology crosses something out from that list of good things in order for it to work. And in Socialism, one of the things crossed out is freedom. When a person is restricted to do some things or to own some things, he is stripped off of his freedom. And this is done to ensure that some others are not crossed out.

First, let me discuss the first model, and then I will give a detailed structure of the first model.

The people who are in charge of the city, I call them the state. The state owns all farmlands, and all livestock, implying that markets that sell raw food are owned by the state. The state owns all factories, meaning that businesses who want to mass-produce their products will have to sign a contract with the state hence share profits with the state. The state also is in control of giving employment to construction workers, in other words when people want to build something, they have to pay the state for the use of construction workers that can only be given by the state. Jobs that provide civil service are also issued by the state, police officers, firefighters, bodyguards, taxi drivers, electricity, water, telephone. Trash collection is also a job that is only issued by the state. So in the first model, no one can own their own farmlands, livestock, factory. Every job that is seen heinous to do or has something to do with civil service or providing the city with raw food supply, these jobs can only be worked by becoming an employee of the state. And the state will wage them a good sum because these jobs are the jobs that safeguard the needs of the people living in the city. But people are allowed to own houses, transportation, and businesses but not in the early stages of the city being built. It is not possible for the state to accommodate the wants of the people, during the early stages.

The reason for these lines of work that are owned by the state is for the sake that the state will be able to issue money as wages to the people. This is also done as a means so that the money gets returned to the state and does not circulate around the people in such a way that allows the existence of the super-rich — one who owns a huge sum of money, to exist. Because private business is allowed in the first model, it makes way for people to own a lot of paper money. And when these businesses try or decide to give their employees a lower wage so that they may have more profits, well, the employees could come and become an employee of the state where the wage is really attractive for one's living standard. And so there is no way a business could wage an employee in an inconsiderate way. In fact, every private business that wants an employee will wage the employee well just so that their employee remains their employee. And this is one of the things that I understand is not possible to be done in a Democracy. Whereas this first model allows a proper wage given to employees by their employer because there is no other way to retain an employee than to wage them at a similar standard or at a higher wage level than compared to the wages the state gives its employees.

In order that the city becomes a successful city that fully uses an enclosed economic system towards its people, we have to ensure that the city has everything it needs, within its surrounding areas, to sustain life, which is food and water, and also including other necessities needed for an early modern civilization to thrive — electricity, telephone lines, sewage system, buildings, and infrastructure. We cannot be dependent on another city or country for our food supply. The moment the basic needs of a human being is dependent on someone else, we are dead because the people in the world will have leverage over us. The number one thing we need to own ourselves is the food supply. The city that will help the people, will go down the drain if we do not have more than enough to feed ourselves. We need more than enough of our food supply in order for this system to work. If possible we need twice the amount of food to ensure a working city that does not crumble halfway. It is only through the excess amount of food that we have that will allow the state to do trade with other countries, in the early stages of the city. In the later stages of the city, the state will be able to do more trade with other cities and countries, by other means of exchange that will be supplied by the people living in the city.

The above describes the first model and how the people will live and how the people can get outside goods and furniture to come into their city. Both the people and the state will be able to communicate with one another with ease so that the needs of the people and the wants of the people, can be met. This is how I see the city I had envisioned to be. A government body that has no other agenda other than doing what could provide more for the people and providing for the people their wants and needs.

Before moving on, I would like to explain the ownership of the factories and the few good reasons why all and every type of factory should be owned by the state. Factories here means all types of factories: food production factories that mass produces potato chips & snacks and other consumable goods, packaging factories that provides packaging, factories that create our plastic bags, plastic bottles for every drinking products, factories for building materials, factories for mass production of electronics and other non-food products, etc. Simply state that every private business that wants to mass-produce either consumable goods or non-consumable products, will need to pay the state in order to mass-produce their products. This way, (1) money is returned to the state, (2) the state can ensure that foods are safe to be eaten, (3) the state can ensure the packaging hygiene and the information (expiration date, calories, and such) included on the packaging concerning the food to be correct. The important thing is that the state can ensure this and that by owning the factories, all of which is done for the good sake of all the people, coexisting in the society.

Under democracy, we hear conspiracy theories deduce that although the government is above the people, there are those rich people who are above the government. But under a socialist state, because of the restriction that prevents people from being super-rich, and so the evil that money can bring about in a person doesn't happen. This is also the case because the paper used as money in an enclosed economic system does not actually carry value. It only carries value because the state issued it to having value. That is why it is unusable outside the place it is issued to have value.

Now, let's move on to the structure of the city. First, we need land to build the city upon and we need land to farm crops and herd animals. We need land with a water supply to drink and for our crops and animals as well. And then we need the animals, the seeds for crops, and the equipment to pave the way towards our water supply. After this we need the people who will do these three jobs and also a chef job is needed to cook the raw food into food that we could eat. In the early stages, the state would need teachers, doctors, and chefs to be state-owned employees as well. All these people will not be able to choose any jobs other than these jobs that are needed to get the city started. And their wages are not low fees. The state acknowledges every job as a necessity to the building of the city and so pays them high fees. The state will then tell the people that they should keep their money so that they may buy houses when we come to the stage of having houses set up. This way, people won't buy food more than they can take in which would waste the food we ourselves produce. Aside from this, we need factories to create construction materials and prepare the construction workers to start building temporary shelters for the people to live in. And so the first few jobs that are available will be: those taking care of the crops, those taking care of the animals, those in charge of transporting our water, those in charge of distributing our raw produce to the state-owned chefs, the chefs themselves who will cook for the people in exchange for money that will go straight back to the state, state-owned doctors who will care for the sick, state-owned teachers who will teach the children that also came with their parents, daycare centers to look after children, the people in charge of thinking of other jobs that could be done by people who somehow can't work in any of the early jobs available, construction workers who will build the shelters and simple sewage systems, the factory workers who will supply construction building materials. And we may need to think about where our source of electricity will be coming from before we plan the city and its location.

Once we have a hold of our food supply, we will then, start on the city and the transportation from the city to the early stages workplaces. We'll have to build residential apartments first to save space and then followed by hospitals and schools. And those who can afford the houses will be able to be the first to move into them, in the city.

A year after the first batch of people start residing in the city, we will then be able to build community blocks and start allowing private businesses (which may probably be restaurants first), to be set up. We would also need the state-owned markets to be built in the city first during the time of the first building of residential areas so that people could start buying and cooking in their homes, in the cities. Not to mention that the residential areas would need a sewage system, electric grids, and telephone lines to be in place. We would probably need professionals to outlay the layout of how we want the city to be before we start working on the city.

After all these are in our grasp, we will then be ready to expand and come up with other jobs and entertainment to provide the people with. From here on out, the reader could imagine adding other things to this city because we would then already have a working city. There is one more thing that I forgot to mention. Because we are eating off our own food supply without leaning onto other parties and the money printed out is actually money that does not base itself on anything, hence does not lead to inflation, and so taxation of the people in the city can be taken out of the picture altogether.

If you are wondering why inflation doesn't happen, the answer could be found in the previous chapters. But to put it simply, without causing a hassle for the reader, let me state it here. Inflation happens because we allow ourselves to be in an open economic system, which has its benefits of direct trade with other countries that can be done by individuals in the country. But in order for our currency to be trusted as a means of payment or to be trusted to have value in the world market, the currency we use, need to have the same basis as to how all the other countries base their currencies on. And so all countries use that same thing or in other words, all the countries in the open market, based their currencies on some same object of principal, in which back in the day used to be gold. But at this current time, it is no longer gold but something else. I have no idea what it is. If you are asking who made that transition, one of the American presidents did it and the whole world just seems to follow with the transit to the new standard. But what I do know, is that that new standard, whatever it is, hence defines the exchange rate between the currencies of two countries. To my understanding, gold can be mined and be added to the vault that stores the gold but that new standard, simply state, can't be mined and be added to the vault. And so that new standard is a fixed medium which cannot be added to. Using a fixed medium, we inflate the currency by printing paper money, more than the value of that fixed medium. And so under this understanding, which has an indirect correlation with one another, inflation happens because individuals in the country want to have the power to do trade with other countries or other peoples in other countries, so as to attain wealth for oneself, and much wealth leads to having power. [In 2021, as the writer, I find this paragraph quite strange with regard to the part 'hence defines the exchange rate', where my current knowledge is that the exchange rate between currencies is defined by the export & imports of a country as discussed in the written chapters of 2021. But I allow this paragraph to exist to let both the reader and myself know what my previous knowledge of it was.]

(Now, if this is truly the case, then it would mean to say that, the transition from the gold standard to this new unknown standard, was orchestrated by somebody or group of people that was able to push the then president to make that transition, for the sake of selfish power.)

Or rather in a better way of putting it, inflation happens because we want a much simpler process to do trade with other countries other than the use of barter which is unreliable. And so in order for trade to be done fairly and as a means of reliability, every currency of those countries wanting to be a part of the open economic system needs to base their currency on a fixed medium that is shared between all the countries using the system. And then because of that fixed medium in place, whenever we need to print money to add to the money in circulation within our society, inflation happens because we print more money than that of the value of the medium, our currency is based on.

And so inflation [I probably meant to say 'fluctuations of the economy'] happens because there seems to be the need to do trade with other countries or with individuals of those other countries. This is why I propose a sustainability type of city so that we do not lean on someone else but on ourselves.

Another thing the reader could understand is this. An open economic system helps businessmen strive to obtain whatever they want. But if you are a person who just wants to get a good and decent-paying job without ever opening a business, living in an open economic system, will drain you out in the future. Honestly speaking, I feel that an open economic system is a playing field for businessmen.

And so the answer to the question why doesn't inflation happen in an enclosed economic system is because, we lean on ourselves for our basic needs as a human being and the people in that enclosed economic system, trusts the state to be the one who will get them what they need and may want by means of trade with other countries done only by the state and not through any individual that is inside the city. Actually what Socialism does with all its restrictions, is the creation of the ability to set up a local currency that defies the logical understanding that the whole world has, with regards to the idea that printing money should lead to inflation. It's difficult to explain. But inflation doesn't happen because everyone cares for one another and understands their roles that they need to play in society, respectively, in order for a successful working, harmonious city. That is why inflation doesn't happen. [As for this paragraph, I have explained what was difficult to explain in the chapters written in 2021. But this explanation is also to be noted. It seems that as you grow older, you end up being able to explain things more clearly in your writings.]

Now, for the understanding of the second model, which uses an enclosed economic system, that is fully restrictive towards its people, please refer to the next chapter of this book which is also the chapter where I disclose the city that I had envisioned for a long time that will ensure the prosperity of every individual where the whole city is one family that partakes in societal participation and understands that every individual has a role to play to ensure the lasting survival of the city. And that one big family is also at the same time working together as a single corporation that provides products for the state to sell abroad and hence be able to purchase whatever the people needs and may want to have. [Remember, this is the second last chapter of an unpublished book I wanted to publish back in 2018. A wholly restrictive model can be found by reading, the '**Third Grand Chapter**' in this book.]

People who still call this a pipe dream, let me ask you this question. First of all, what do I need which I stated as a necessity of a city? Land. Can I be given the land for free? If the country would like to help the people, there is the possibility that land can be given for the building of the city for the sake of these refugees and what they could offer the country, in the future, as a token of thanks for the city given to them.

After land what do I need that I also stated? Crops and food supply for the people living inside the city. First of all, can I get seed and all the other things needed for manual labor to produce crops, fruits, vegetables? Maybe I can even get them for free so that the people can work the ground to produce raw food for themselves without asking to share the food supply of the country that helps them.

As for meats and milk and eggs, can I get the animals that could give the people these 3 things, for free? Maybe a big no. But surely I am allowed to purchase these animals from the country, right? And so all I need to do is find the money to purchase the animals needed for the people in the new city. The people would then be able to herd the animals themselves and be able to feed themselves in the long run.

Once we have the food supply we get chefs, around the world, who would want to help the struggling citizens of the new city and also get paid at the same time to live and work in the city.

The next thing I need is, construction works. For that, the people will need to know how to make the materials used for buildings and roads. For our own buildings, we'll have our own factories that will provide the building materials. And even the construction workers will be the refugees themselves doing the job. The only things that they would need would be the proper knowledge to do those construction building work.

Next, we will have teachers and doctors, and also build buildings for those 2 jobs that will educate and take care of the people within the new cities.

Wages will then be given to all the people working in the city, by the city itself. The wages will be more than enough to feed oneself. The city will make sure of it. As long as those of the working-age work in the city, in areas the city needs them to be, the city will be able to provide them good wages without worrying about inflation ever happening.

If you have read until this part and can see hope, re-read the solution and understand it. If you still see it as a pipe dream, all this book offers you is information about our surroundings without any solution to it. And so if you bought this book looking for a solution, this book has failed you. But if you can see the picture as I see it, then this book has provided you with something worth something. All that's left is to accommodate the idea into the fruition of it. You can start by getting a body of people in your country that understands this idea and together bring this idea to the attention of your government with the hope of being aided by your government to do this good act for the sake of both the people who are in need of aid and for the sake of the future returns this city can bring to the country that sponsors its existence.

What I hope by sharing this idea to the world is that every country would allow the building of one city in their country, either for the sake of their own people that are striving to live and/or for the sake of the refugees that are looking for a new home. Let them work towards a new city to call home, let them work for it. This way, they do not disturb the living standards of the people living in the country of their sponsorship, ensuring that burdens that come upon the people of the country are kept to a minimum and so there is no reason for the people of the country to kick the refugees out because the money given to the people working in the new city is a totally different currency than the one used in the country and so there is no effect at all economically speaking.

Just give these people who are in need, the nets to catch fish, and they will build their own economic system and prosper. All that can be done, with a small investment their sponsors will need to provide them, to start off with.

ANOTHER NOTE: What I give to the world by taking a few of the people from an open economy, to living in a closed economy, is the easing of the suffering of the people of them I take away and also the prosperity of those I do not take away is leveled up because of the decrease in the number of people in their local society. This can be seen as similar to the reduction of a country's population and what it does to the local economy. If the rich want to be richer whilst living in an open economic system, the building of that closed economic city can help you make that happen. Not only does this reduce problems for the country that implements this but also by allowing the city built, the country is investing in a sort of safety net that can be of use in the future.

I keep on hearing stories that the rich want to get richer. And they do all sorts of things to chase after wealth. Be it legal or illegal. Be it Eco-friendly or not. Be it disruptive of the lives of others or not. No matter what happens to others, as long as they can be rich, they go for it. And this justifies the phrase that money is the root of all evil. The use of cheaper yet harmful ingredients in food, just to take down business competitions. They do foul play. All these just to chase paper that is of value.

Money is to be used as a medium of exchange. Once money is more than just a medium of exchange, when money becomes a sign of power or when through the withholding of money, it causes others hardships, that system should no longer be valid to be used. Because money should only play one role and that is to be a much reliable form of barter, and that, is a reliable medium of exchange. Once it becomes something more than what it was intended to be, we have to reevaluate that system or we may have to change that system because with regard to money becoming a way to have power over others, the people end up being given the probability that they will suffer. If everyone has a good heart and understands the effect of their actions, even if we allow money to be power, I doubt that the people will suffer. But this is not the case. If just one person does bad, the whole country will be affected by this one bad person who uses the availability of the equation that 'money is power' to cause himself to be above others. That is why building a city from scratch is the goal I intended to do.

My goal is not to change that already ongoing system. My goal is to take the people out and build a system for them that is independent of the current ongoing system. And that system that I plan on building for them is a system where paper money is just acting as a means of exchange, nothing more. Where (1) there is no power in money because that paper that is issued is not based on a value that has material worth but rather it is based on a value of people working together. [Yes!] If the people do not work together in the city, respectively doing their job for their society, that paper that is issued will be of no value. And (2) the withholding of money does not cause hardships because every time a person is paid for a job that is owned by the state, the state prints new money to pay the employee, and inflation doesn't happen in an enclosed economic system. [Yes!]

In other words, the city that I envisioned is a city where the people living in the society, know and understand what needs to be done to keep the city going. They do their respective jobs that are supervised by the state and they serve one another by doing those jobs. The state who oversees and knows the big picture will tell the society, what job the city needs more employees in, and to have people want to switch jobs, the state will offer a higher pay for the job in which the city is in need of. This way, the city acts as a family because they do what is needed, not for the survival of their individual self, but for the survival of the whole city. And those that receive the lowest pay, that is paid out by a state-owned job, is equaled to a sum of 30 steaks of 400 grams each.

The wicked want instant gratification. Those who are not wicked but are of the opposite will certainly be the ones who would want to endure hardships for a better future. Before the city is built or during the process of its building, restrictions are in place. The restrictions are made known with reasonings to the people. Once the city is built, some wicked hearts may come in along with other people into the city. But those wicked men will not be able to do wickedness because of the restrictions. And so if they want to live in the city, although they have evil hearts, the manifestation of evil into actions is made limited. The restrictive system that I have in mind does not allow anyone to oppress anyone. If good people are restricted in such a way that they are unable to harm anyone, wicked men will see this and shudder. In the end, the wicked men, who maybe became wicked after being oppressed by someone else in the open economy, will be able to revert of their ways for the better, if they choose to stay. [Hallelujah!]

Those who have hardships living in an open market economy where an individual lives for himself, by himself. No matter where we are in the open economy, no matter our job description, no matter how many friends we have, we all live individual lives because the money that we have is the money we earn our individual selves. And because we earned it all by our individual selves, we have in ourselves, the unconscious understanding that we live for ourselves, by ourselves. Whereas the economy that I envisioned for the city is that the money we have, is the money that is of value only because every single one of us in that city makes it so. When a person is individualistic, he becomes, unbeknownst to himself, selfish and ignorant of the needs of others. But when we see that if we don't do our part, the stranger on the street suffers, and if that stranger does not do his part, we suffer whereas the system that we live inside of, is strict and just in such a way there is no other way to live than to do our part, we are made to do our part with the knowledge and understanding of why we have to do so. This is somewhat difficult to explain but the thing is this, the system affects how the people live inside the system and how the people live inside that system affects the lives of their surrounding peoples.

If you believe in a place called Heaven. You will understand that in Heaven only good people will be there and so you will have freedom there. But while we are on the Earth, the only way we could simulate a happy society is to be restrictive onto all the people, may they be good or bad, have restrictions placed on both of them. People may say that I treat the good, the same way I treat the bad. But if we were to understand that the bad are not the ones who will want to spend 10 years building the city, therefore we should understand that it is 'the bad' that will be given the same treatment, given to the good.

In some of the world's religions, there is a story that tells of how the Creator gave the first man 'free will'. This is the will to choose between evil and good. This means to say that the Creator gave the first man the ability to choose where he wants to end up in. Does he want to live freely without any restrictions, which may cause him to stumble and end up doing something that unbeknownst to him, endangers his salvation? Or does he want to live a life where he observes himself and restricts himself so as to carefully walk to ensure that he keeps everything in check so as to receive a sure salvation?

What I want is peace and harmony for the people. What I want is that the people consciously care for one another. And the only way I could think of achieving such a society, in such a world filled with competition, power-greedy, wicked men that end up affecting the world in such a way that those who do not hold tightly to their religions or good values will end up becoming wicked men themselves, can only be done by building a new city that imposes restrictions and Socialistic values to the people.

If you want to live in a system that gives you freedom, be prepared because not only do you get freedom but the wicked in heart who lives inside the system is also allowed that same freedom you have and that wickedness, once manifested into actions may cause people like yourself to suffer. Because wickedness will use whatever it can use to do wickedness to others. Let me say this again. Because money is no longer a means of exchange but also a means of power over others, money issues, for us who just want to live a good honest life, is right around the corner. Wickedness exploits everything and uses everything to its advantage without caring for anyone else. Freedom becomes problematic because we allow freedom in our society. **Once we understand this, we will choose restrictions over freedom, not as a punishment to ourselves but for the sake of ensuring peace and harmony in our society.**

One of the last short topics after the last chapter of, my previous Socialist book that was never published :

(1) THE RICH MAY want riches. Riches lead to power. Power leads to control. Control could mean, control of the market. Finally, they could end up having control over peoples around the world. If this is the agenda, in order that they may have control over the people. The only thing that I could think of, why they want the control of the people is so that they may transit the world into using a system that they have designed. And if they do not have control over the people, this transit will not be able to take place and so they thrive to achieve the control of the people. By making sure that money is inflatable and by making sure that all the countries follow and be a part of their open economic system, they make it so that money equals power. And then they do all sorts of things to gain power so as to have control.

And so from the moment, the gold standard was replaced, and the whole world followed the American system, we were all entrapped into their agenda of allowing ourselves to be controlled by them in order that they may issue a system that they have designed to be used globally.

(2) MY PERSPECTIVE IS that if the people in a country don't like the constitution, or don't like the base foundations of the country, that people shouldn't be oppressed, but be allowed to leave the country. If China doesn't want Christians, then allow those Chinese who are Christians to go to another country that will accept their belief in their religion. Those who feel that their homeland has turned them into becoming a minority or their government have allowed some things to become law because of a single person's dislike or find it to be unconstitutional, this means to say that your government no longer sides with you and you should plan on finding another country that may allow you to live the way you previously lived.

My point is, I don't like the oppression of the people. If the country doesn't want the people, instead of oppressing them, give them away to another country that will accept them. Staying in a country that does not respect you, will bring about distress, and they will continue to oppress you.

(3) FOR A SIDE NOTE, America was founded under Christianity that abhors to the God of the Israelites. And so those who dislike Christianity should be allowed to choose another country to go to and live in that other country rather than to stay in America and complain about not liking the Christian values that have existed in the country for many years, even before they were born. But if the government of

the American people, chooses to side with the people who find Christian values as unconstitutional, therefore although America is your homeland for many generations, I suggest that the Christians in America leave their homeland and find another country that allows your worship of God. For your government, once they have sided against Christian values will not revert back into siding with Christian values. For once they have allowed evil into their hearts and evil has a grip on that person, that person will not revert. And it is best that you leave now for although you have the right to revolt against the government for siding against Christian values, you will lose the physical battle and your government will oppress you with military force. They will go to this extent because they have sided against you by no longer accepting Christian values as the norm of the American people. They will hate you because they first hated Him and you chose Him over the world.

(4) SOMETIMES, people use the internet for learning and understanding, some other time for music, games, and entertainment. There are countries that restrict media and the internet to an extent but for me personally, I do not intend on restricting the use of it unless there are some things that could result badly for others around them if we allow such content to be received by the people. Countries that do not allow media into their countries are afraid of some sort of revolution that could topple the government. But I do not fear the harm to myself. I fear more the disruptions of a

society in harmony. I am not some person whose interest is in himself but a person just really wanting the happiness of the people. Therefore I do not mind people bad-mouthing me or my ideology. As long as I have given the understanding to the people of a better way of life and I have shown the world of its success, nothing else matters except for the disruptions of those who want to live under my ideology. If you hate my ideology, do not crush it, go out there and build yourself a new city and place your ideology as its foundation. Do not bring sadness to the people happily living in it for likewise do I intend on building a new city rather than changing an already going city because change will bring sadness to some. Whereas my goal is not sadness to some. I am not a businessman. My goal is happiness to all.

III. The Reason For My Writing Of This Book (Revamped From The Words Written In 2017)

INFORMATION CONCERNING THE AUTHOR, COMMENTARIES & HIS LAST WORDS

T HE YEAR I decided to write and finish this book that consists of ideas and information accumulated from 2008 is the year 2021. I have been wanting to write this book for 7 years or so and in 2021, there was a 4 months program to writing a book. I joined that program and this book is published (hopefully) also in that same year (because it depends on the publisher and other stuff).

This book consisting of topics is a book written with the intention of giving knowledge to readers concerning the aspects of Socialism. Bluntly speaking, I see Socialism as a way out for human beings that have difficulties living in this modern, ever-changing world. Honestly, I believe that

Socialism isn't for the rich because the rich do not have economic problems. One of the aspects of Socialism is its ability to give life & purpose to every individual in society. The purpose individuals will have will be for the sake of the continual existence of the whole society itself. The life that they will have will be a life where they can work and eat and live, all the while be able to spend more quality time with their families and friends. No longer does the individual take on the weight of carrying his own burden but as a collective, our burdens are made lighter because of the existence of the collective.

Up to today, coming to the end of 2021, with me being 31 years old this same year, I still haven't been able to successfully succeed through means of personally securing funds for the thing that I wanted to do. I had business plans that could provide me with some funding but my wage until 2017 was just enough for my own living. I am one of those employees who were paid not below the government standard but still below the average sum given to employees who had the same job as I have throughout a period of 4 years from 2013. The reason for the writing of this book was to give an understanding to the socialistic dream that I hope to achieve, to give knowledge concerning the current world, ask for aid either through discussions followed by funding or getting people to acknowledge my existence and maybe be able to work with the current administration or any future ones to bring about small cities that will give a better living to some of the country's people.

IV. Improvements On This Book

I BELIEVE THAT many improvements can be made to this book that will bring a better understanding to the audiences reading it and wanting to know more about definitions and terms, also about understanding the philosophy and wisdom behind Socialism that tries to bring about a workaround for society in order to prevent societal breakdowns and other individual problems that may build up in a particular individual and turn him into a bad person which perhaps will become a bad influence to society.

This book warns the world that every individual life matters because all you need is one man and through that one man, the whole world may plunge into darkness. To care for the world and the people living in the world is to care for the happiness of every individual person in existence at that given point in time. This is what leaders are supposed to do

— providing a means that may accommodate the assimilation of mankind into a society that does not seek to ruin itself.

I have tried to provide the understanding towards that goal but may have been lacking in some parts.

To tell someone a piece of advice or information is simple. But to bring him / her to the understanding thereof, you may have to open the mind of that person and lead him / her in a step-by-step process. That is the journey intended by the writing of this book. To bring about a perspective that has been branded evil by the evils in society.

The building blocks of society are not the ability of talented people. Talented people, rich people, people of status, clever people, creators, or inventors: these are not the building blocks of society. The building blocks of a society are the yearnings for the existence of the society itself. Societies are formed through the collaboration and affection of one person to the other, building the society together. It is only after the building of societies that we forget how society was built which leads to the fall of society into the many states of hardships.

For an everlasting kingdom to exist, we may need an everlasting king that represents wisdom itself so that the values of the king may embody the citizens and prevent the cycle of history from repeating itself. But whenever there exists a person in society that dislikes the values of the king, with much incitement caused by an external entity or group of people, a revolution will be around the corner. In the case of the Christian belief of the 1000 years, that revolution will be met with Godly intervention.

V. My Take On Happenings On The World Stage (From Early 2021, Moving Forward)

INFORMATION CONCERNING THE AUTHOR, COMMENTARIES & HIS LAST WORDS

ON ONE SIDE, there is a Marxist Ideology and on the other extreme end, there is America who wants to impose its views of Democracy onto the world. The way I see it, both these countries have conflicting interests and values, and understandings of how the world should work. Because both intend to influence the world towards conforming to their good respective values from their own respective perspectives, we can see some form of conflict on the world stage.

People say the Communist-Marxist country is on the offensive. This statement is wrong. Capitalist America is the one on the offensive and has been on the offensive for a long time, since world war 2. Why I use Capitalist to describe

America shouldn't be a surprise anymore because Capitalists (business people with self-interest) are found within Democracy. The people of America are democratic but the players behind America's decisions are Capitalists in nature. And like I said in order for a person to interact with others, that person needs to get them into the same ocean as he is. That ocean is Democracy and Free, Open Markets. America has been offensive for a long time, getting people into that same ocean so that those players can manipulate the economy, and get what they want, when they want it; because once everyone is in the same ocean, or once every country is on the same boat but in different cabins, those who know how can rise above others and tilt the economies of countries to their favor. Whatever evils can be done in a free country with regard to issues of money and wealth, can also be done on the world stage. In other words, if poverty can come to a man within a country because of someone in that same country, if the world is made to conform to the same system used within that country, poverty in country B can also be caused by someone in country A.

In the previous paragraph, we discussed who is on the offensive all this time. Whereas what Marxist does is not being 'the offensive' but rather is doing what it currently is doing (which seems like an offensive), as a means to secure itself from being vulnerable, of being attacked by Capitalism. The defense mechanism of Marxism on the world stage is to cripple the movements of Capitalism. And the only way they can do so is by somehow being able to control, a part of, if not all of, the global market.

There is a difference between someone attacking because he wants to and someone attacking as a means to defend himself. The goal of the defensive is to wear out the enemy that is doing the blows until they are on the same stamina level or the other option is to hold and endure until the round ends. The good thing about the defensive is that it tends to be able to observe the opponent and if he observes long enough, he will understand the opponent in such a way that he can come with a plan to counter the offensive. The Marxist country that is on the world stage has been enduring and observing how the world works, how Capitalism has been advancing, and the tricks up its (Capitalism's) sleeve. I fear that the moment it counters causing unconsciousness, it will not just stop there but continue to hit the opponent for all the humiliation it had endured. And having ended the opponent, it will cease to stop but continue towards dictating its values on the world stage just as how America has been doing.

In our current era of the late 20th and early twenty-first century, we have been witnessing the battle between Capitalism and those who try to fend off Capitalism. On one side we have those with self-interests and on the other side, we have those who have felt the impacts of Capitalism and its unfair practices and are trying to rise up against it. Where have we seen this same type of dispute other than in the 1800s? I like to see this as the battle between good and evil. In the Christian understanding, we have Satan with his self-interests of popularizing the ability to do whatever he wants (which is found within Democracy and Freedom by the way) and on the other side, we have God who teaches values of co-existence — to love what is good, just, loving, righteous and by doing those things, you are said to have loved God because God represents those things, in other words, his being are all those things combined. And so when you love goodness, you love God because He is goodness itself.

If I could just bluntly say it out, what does the Devil want? In the Christian understanding, the Devil who was previously an angel in heaven, what was the problem that causes him to turn against God? What did he want, that God with all His wisdom, is unwilling to provide? The Devil wants to be God, in other words, he doesn't like the idea of God ruling forever. To the Devil, when God rules forever, that's what he calls authoritarianism or a dictatorship that is not willing to step down and give someone else a try. Simply, the Devil wants Democratic elections in Heaven. The Devil wants freedoms and rights. Why does the Devil want this? God knows it is because the Devil has a rotten agenda therefore in order to do and be able to execute his agenda, he needs both freedom and the required rights (which only can be obtained by allowing freedom first).

In the mortal world, when rights are given based on freedom, the rights can be used to achieve bad agendas. This is a fact in reality and that's what the Devil promotes in our societies.

I believe Christian pastors know that rights and freedom were what the Devil wanted from God but are unwilling to disclose that fact. I believe they know Democracy is yearned for by the Devil to exist in heaven so that he could be free to do what he believes is correct according to him. This is the same reasoning people promote Democracy in our mortal societies — to allow values of different perspectives to exist. It's like the world is driven by the Devil to want Democracy because of all the things that Democracy allows — the freedom to go against God yet be protected by the laws of Democracy, in other words, the freedom to go against God yet have a feeling of correctness. The Devil wants to bring the Godly realm into the box of Democracy where within Democracy and with the values found within it, the Devil can achieve his agenda.

The Devil wants to prove God wrong, that given the temptations of the world and the freedom to chase after evil, the people will choose evil rather than goodness. But God counters by telling the Devil, "Let them be for My people are those who will choose goodness no matter the temptations of evil thereof."

By being able to view self-interest as something that exists even in the history of Christianity, we could authenticate Christianity as one of those religions that may be true and that both the Christian God and the heavenly realm might in fact exist.

Lastly, I want to ask the readers to view the world and see that if they can tell me that I am wrong. That self-interest isn't the problem of societal breakdowns. That self-interest does not exist. That self-interest can be used to shape the societies of the world and bring good values to the people. Is anyone able to say all these things? If not then if Socialist minds (which are human minds) are trying to prevent self-interest (to the utmost ability from the logical, intellectual mind of the Socialist) for the sake of an everlasting future for human civilization, why do people hate us? People hate us because they were guided into hating us. And the people who guided them, closed all the good understandings found within Socialism and make it look like Socialism is the wicked one and they show (to people) that the ideal and ideas found within Socialism yearn to do evil towards society. This is what has been happening, ladies and gentlemen. Now you know.

VI. Contributions To The Disbelief Towards A Form Of God That Marx May Have Also Believed In

INFORMATION CONCERNING THE AUTHOR, COMMENTARIES & HIS LAST WORDS

WHAT I HAVE down below are 5 statements that Atheists, people of Science, and the logical minds of the world, believe hinder themselves from believing in God. In every single statement, the reader can find my intellectual findings to state otherwise.

1. The Problem Of (Allowed) Evil (Happening In Society) - A Major Objection For Existence Of God.

[I'd like to try and disprove this statement.]

HOW DO YOU counter evil? You counter evil by having good values.

God's being represents good values. God does not like evil. But whether he allows evil or not is something I cannot logically answer.

From my logical understanding, God does not have control over evil. Why do I say this? I believe in the following statement. Evil itself inevitably exists because of **a choice of self-interest, made by the self**.

Evil exists based on the choice, made by the self. As long as there is choice, evil can exist. The problem here is why did God give mankind the ability of choice when he knew choice may cause evil to appear?

God is a being that has a choice and He chooses goodness. Once again, logically speaking from the perspective of the mind of a human being (which cannot comprehend the theory that God is goodness itself), i present to you the following statement. God out of his wisdom, must have made the choice of goodness and because of this He created mankind and gave them the ability of making choices **in the hopes that** they choose goodness over evil just as how God Himself chooses goodness over evil.

God wants a society that knows what is right and what is wrong yet chooses what is right because it is the best choice a wise man can make. **So,** evil is not something that can be allowed or cannot be allowed. Logically speaking, it is only present because we have a choice. That is why we need the understanding of good values to make the right choices.

The moment free will was given to us, the moment mankind has the freedom to choose how they want to live or how they want to go about their lives, we become prone to doing evil. We can only counter this behavior, found in every being that has a conscience, by giving that being a reason for being good. Once any being has become 'enlightened' on why being good is better than doing evil, that being still has to make the choice of being good and then he becomes good.

This phenomenon is found within every being that has a conscience. The angels have a conscience, God has a conscience, we as human beings have a conscience.

I believe God, in all his wisdom, wanted us to choose goodness over evil that is why we were given a conscience in the first place. A conscience also separates us from being mindless dolls. God wants a kingdom of mindful people that chooses goodness over evil — bringing about a kingdom of everlasting righteousness.

2. The (Allowed) Sufferings Of Man, Is Another Objection For The Existence Of (A Caring) God.

A MAN SUFFERS because of something. There is always a cause. He lost money because he was scammed. A chainsaw accidentally cuts off his left leg causing tremendous pain and shock. He lost his house to the flood and hurricane. He gets hit by a bus and wakes up from a coma ten years later. A judge misjudges a man and sends the man into prison where he ends up molested and raped by other men. A breakup, a divorce, or the death of a loved one. These are the sufferings faced by human beings. Traumatic, financial, emotional, psychological sufferings. These are very heavy burdens on mankind. Talking about these may generate more content than this book itself. But why is God seen as a God who allows these sufferings to befall upon man? I honestly can't answer this one from a logical perspective. But what I can say is, outside the clumsiness and the (conscious or unconscious) self-inflicting harm done by human beings themselves, there are two other sufferings : (1) sufferings from natural disasters and (2) sufferings from the actions of someone else.

For the natural disasters, there are those that are (1) man-made and those that are (2) caused by nature itself. The one caused by nature itself can either be seen as bad luck (by non-believers) or a sign of warning from God (by believers). If the natural disaster caused by nature takes away life, those who believe in God will say that those people must have done something wrong (not in the eyes and understanding of man but in the eyes and understanding of God). Because if (a good) God is in control of nature, then it would be through the means of nature that God chastises man, definitely, for some good reason — maybe according to God he or she has done something despicable in God's eyes that no one else knows about (which comes down to the reasoning of God Himself as to 'how much evil is too much evil').

God can only control what he is in control of. If God respects His own creations and gave mankind the choice to make their choices and those choices that were made, inflicted sufferings on someone else, the reason God does not intervene would be to bring about the understanding to both parties, concerning choice and the effects and consequences of the made choice, which was caused, witnessed, and felt by the transgressor himself.

(Let me pause here and add that when God created man, because he created man based on Himself, based on his image and likeness, which actually mean that the creations should 'unconsciously' have some if not all of God's good values, therefore when a person does wrong to others there must be some type of resistance within his being that informs him that what he is doing is wrong. Some form of guilt is felt when a man who is **unconsciously** good-natured does something against that nature. That's the scoop I could think of to help with this topic.)

The reason God does not intervene when a man suffers from an action (directly or indirectly) caused by another person, all comes down to the goal of God for allowing choice to exist. And the intended goal of (a good and caring) God from a logical perspective is to bring about a feeling of guilt that may hopefully change the transgressor's opinions and values regarding the effects of his actions. In simpler terms, because the creator wants all of mankind (His creations) to have a good understanding of goodness, as to be able to be accepted into Heaven (to live with God), **God allows suffering**, not for the sake of the one suffering but rather **for the sake of the transgressor** — the one who chooses to transgress. Because it is in most cases, if not all, that **the transgressor is the one lacking in understanding** and God wants him to understand by allowing him to cause someone else to suffer.

As for the ones suffering, God, in turn, blesses them. And it is strongly asked of them to forgive the people who inflicted pain unto them or persecute them because once again the goal of God is the hope that all flesh enters into the Kingdom of God. Those who endure suffering and yet prays for their persecutors are doing God a big favor to remind God of His goals with regard to the creation of mankind. Those who forgive and pray for their enemies will surely be rewarded by God.

Allow me to echo the important parts. The goal of God is for mankind to have understanding. If God intervenes whenever his clone makes a mistake, in such a way that before that clone rapes another person, God supernaturally comes down and stops the rape from happening, then the sinner will have no understanding of consequences that appear because of bad actions. But every time God allows his clone to cause someone else to suffer, God wants his evil clone to gain understanding in the hopes that that evil clone becomes a good clone after some time. But if at the end of the life of that evil clone, that clone still delights in doing evil, God will punish that clone by throwing that clone into an everlasting furnace of burning sulfur where that evil clone will suffer forever and ever.

In other words, God wants all of mankind to have understanding, choose goodness over evil, and then get a first-class ticket to go to heaven. God wants to give the evil people living in this world as many chances to change their life as He can give. After giving people many chances to change their life, after giving those wicked people beautiful women to marry, after giving those wicked people wealth, after giving those wicked people wonderful careers, and even after all the good things God has given them, if they still choose to do evil, then no one can call God unrighteous for sending those wicked people into the everlasting fire.

God does not want anyone to perish and it is for this very reason that when a person suffers, God does not intervene in hopes that the one who causes the suffering will one day realize that he is wrong and then change his way of life and finally save himself from the everlasting fire.

3. The Lack Of Intellectual Facts From Modern-Day Example, To Justify The Existence Of God.

THE DIFFICULT GOAL of realizing Socialism is a modern-day example (that was thought by intellectual wise human beings) that represents what the society of Heaven will look like.

If God exists and that God is a good God (or claimed to be goodness itself), and He indeed brought about mankind on the earth, then there is a reason, a good reason as to what He wanted for mankind. For as long as we can connect the logical facts that intend to bring about His goal for mankind, (and connect it) with the happenings of life, in the lifespan of a human being, that can be seen and understood to accommodate that ultimate goal, we can deduce given the hypothesis of the existence of God that there is a truthful understanding in that statement.

A hypothesis is a scientific way to understand something where there is a lack of evidence thereof. And if the hypothesis can be proven, then, that hypothesis could be true or if there is no flaw in the understanding of the world given the hypothesis, then that hypothesis must be true. The main hypothesis here are 3 things : (1) God exists, (2) God is good, (3) God created the earth, mankind, and everything else on the earth. The sub hypothesis consists of 4 things : (1) There is a dwelling place of God, (2) God has heavenly subjects, (3) Heavenly subjects has the ability of choice, (4) The rebellion of heavenly subjects took place that brought about the existence of the Devil, evil spirits and the forces which are opposed to the characters and also opposed to the will of God.

If there is a dwelling place of God where there are heavenly subjects that have the ability of choice, **then there is the possibility** that a rebellion could have happened. And when a rebellion or betrayal happens, a single group splits into two (or multiple) groups having different views, some or most (if not all) of which are views that are in opposition to the views of the other group(s). With this in mind, because an opposition of angelic beings exists (given the 4th sub hypothesis that a rebellion could have happened, because of the other 3 sub hypothesis), this could bring about the explanation for why some of the things that happen in the world does not make sense where we end up believing that God has two extreme values (one good and the other bad), whereas the truth of the matter is that there is an opposition made possible by the subjects of God (that were from the heavenly realm) going against God.

So with the existence of 3 main and 4 sub hypotheses, in order to check if those hypotheses are true, questions can then be thrown to test the hypothesis. God still is committed to reaching His (good) goal for creating mankind, even when there is an opposition. **So**, what can happen (to the creations of God on the earth) if there is an opposition to God (by the heavenly subjects of God)? To understand that we must ask ourselves what does the group doing the opposition want to achieve. They want to thwart the plans of God; they want to prove that God and His worldview is wrong; because once they can prove that God is wrong, they could tell God, "See I told you this will happen, please step down. Because you as God is wrong about this and that, and so now let me be God for a change." It all comes down to the opposition wanting to prove God wrong because the opposition has a conflicting view of the world (which could be based on the error of God as to allowing choice in the first place, in other words, the opposing angels could be saying to God that He shouldn't have given the ability to choose in the first place because if God gives the ability to choose, any of them above could make anyone of those creations down below to succumb to the wrong choice and so to justify that God, in all his wisdom, made the wrong decision when he created mankind, the opposing angels which represents the powers and principalities in high places because of their knowledge and sheer will to prove God wrong which gives them the might and determination to be able to think of various ways to prove God wrong, just like how we see bad human beings find different ways to reach their goal ignoring the damage that harms someone else while yearning strongly to reach their goal, it is in this same way that the opposing angels become the powers and principalities in high places, using all their understanding and shaping the human beings to hate

God and bringing various understandings of evil to the world, and then come to the courts of God and accuse the human beings living down below of various faults while at the same time providing God with their inductive findings to justify that their case is true and correct; Sadly in the case of the Bible character named Job whose story could justify the reasoning to other cases happening to anyone living on the earth, in the case of Job, the Devil came to God and asked God for permission to try and see if he could make Job curse God by using all of his wits he could possibly find, in which once again sadly, because God knows that He is never wrong in decision making, allows the Devil to do whatever he can to try and make Job curse God, and happily did the Devil went down and kill the children of Job + make him lose his livestock + make him lose his wife + make him to reason with himself if he truly deserves what he received despite believing having lived a devout and righteous life in the eyes of God, but at the end of the struggles of Job, he did not once curse God, he did make God angry because he said a statement of self-defence with a pinch of pride having been pushed to a corner and not knowing what else to do, which angers God, but in the end the Devil never did make Job curse God; and because of this story of Job, when someone in our life, like a spouse or family member passes away for some reasons, there is a possibility that the Devil went to God and God in turn allowed the Devil to try and prove his point by indirectly ending the life of people and indirectly causing hardships to people just to state a point to God; but if God is indeed good and allows the Devil to prove a point, therefore all those people that were indirectly killed by the Devil will be compensated in accordance to the goodness of God). That is how we can explain the unexplainable things that happen in the world where a good God is supposed to exist.

Coming back to the first paragraph in this topic, there is a coming new Heaven (this is a second Heaven because the first Heaven has been corrupted by the Devil and those other forces) which is a place where God has made it clear that only those who have a choice and with that choice chooses to be good, will be able to enter. Socialism, in the same manner, tries to have everyone conform to goodness and sets up a Kingdom for like-minded people to co-exist. The end goal of both the new Heaven and Socialist utopian dream is to have a society with one mindset which is a mindset conforming to good values that seek to bring about an everlasting incorruptible kingdom where the inhabitants themselves are incorruptible because of their wisdom which allows them to know that evil is indeed a bad thing and will lead to unwanted consequences. But the process by which both God and the minds of logical Socialists achieve that goal is different.

From the Socialist perspective (as human beings), with the intellect and wisdom of a human being, because there exists a form of evil seen and witnessed by the human eyes and understood by the human mind, the best way is to bring about a sustainable city environment which will attract people and then set up the rules that restrict freedom and then give the understanding and reasoning as to why those restrictions are in place, and then have the state care and love the people and provide the people with wants and needs and at the same time develop a personal relationship with the people so as to help every individual know that the state is always there for them, and this will bring about an effect where when the society has matured and is filled with wisdom that was developed over the years by understanding the ways of the ideology, brings about a sense to love one another because they were previously loved and cared for by the state. Having reached that level of responsibility, the state can then slowly remove itself and allow the society, where each person understands the needs of their fellow neighbors, be able to lead itself as a collective without the need of a governing body (that may in the future have self-interest because of the feeling of power that can usually be felt by people in the government body; that is why in all cases, the Socialist who brings about the idea of Socialism, after setting up the city and doing all the things, it would be best that he ensures that the people understand everything that is needed to be understood so that the state can remove itself during his lifespan; because if a wise leader passes leadership to someone else, the man who receives the leadership begets a power that he did not cultivate himself and that power may lead him to self-interest). The end result is, the state, before it removes itself, creates a system where the society follows that system blindly (so as to not change the working system; if a man of wisdom created a system or law, it would be wise to follow it to the letter; a man with curiosity, having been given a system that works, during his tinkering process, will end up deviating society from the functional ways of the system or law that was created for the sole purpose of good governance over that body of people) and with the system itself, people can continue to govern themselves as a collective body conforming to good values of society.

Whereas from the perspective of God, whatever happens, because God who claims to be goodness itself, created mankind from his image and likeness, mankind who wants to call God their God and wants to live with God in a good place filled with good people and good values, will inevitably have to be good no matter what happens so as to be able to one day live with God and amongst those who conform to the characters of God. In other words, God is saying, "If you want to one day, at the end of your lifespan live with me, your creator, then I ask you to live a Godly life following my characteristic traits that I have given to you through my laws that I have given to the **good seeds** of Adam's descendants." In the Christian faith, the laws are the 10 commandments of Moses + the later requirement of believing in Jesus Christ who is known as the son of God where 'son' here means, logically speaking, a person who has the DNA trademark of the parent, in other words, it is to mean that Jesus Christ has the same mindset and values of God.

To understand Jesus Christ and the Christian need for the sacrifice of Jesus Christ to mean something of a big thing in the salvation provided by the Christian religion, we need to ask several questions. One of which is, what makes a being different from other beings aside from the genetic makeup that are the features on the surface? It is the values and mindset the being has. And so when Christ who is one with God (because he is the son of God which scientifically mean to have the same mindset and values of God towards all things, in other words, having consciously understood the unconscious values of Godliness that God has placed upon him, and probably that was placed upon all of us too, to have), died on the cross, having to have lived a Godly life from birth (that is to say without sinning), became a sacrifice that is seen by God as a sacrifice worthy to appease the anger of God at that point in history.

How did I know that God was angry? Because of my own experiences whereby there were instances in my life that I was angry and filled with rage but because I am unwilling to hurt someone else, I (who was 16 years of age at that time) end up crying my anger away. And so when you have a man who is very angry but at the same time doesn't want to cause harm, there is a conflicting reaction going on within the person and the only way to solve the problem within is to ultimately ask for mercy as a last resort. (Another example is you have a man who loves his wife but his wife passed away leaving him with a son. The son breaks something at home that was a memento of the man's cherished wife. When the man found and saw that the object was in pieces, he took a hammer and out of rage, which came from the tremendous love that he had towards his wife, came to his son and was about to hit his son but before the hammer hits the son, he saw his wife's face from the face of his son and instead resolved his anger through tears. The thing to ponder from this story is the understanding of what scientifically happened during the split second. The man sacrificed his current state by means of applying **some form of** mercy.) That 'mercy' that was used to appease the conflicting feelings of God with regard to the behaviors of men towards the God that had promised (their fathers) to love and not annihilate them, became the sacrifice of Jesus Christ which represents the self of God. Jesus Christ knew the will of God and continues to do what he came to do. Because Jesus Christ ends up being sacrificed, as a means of a reward to Jesus Christ, God lifted Christ in such a way that no man can ever come to God (who was angry at man previously but was appeased by Christ's sacrifice on the cross), unless they accepted Jesus Christ as the one who appeased the anger of God. And it is also because of the reason that God no longer wants to hear what the people have to say unless Jesus Christ is accepted by the people when they communicate with God through prayer, that Christ ultimately is seen as God Himself. Because God will not accept you unless you pass through Jesus Christ, therefore the prophecy concerning Jesus Christ that is to be lifted up, is fulfilled. And also the sacrifice of Christ brings about the understanding that if you choose 'sacrifice' and 'forgiveness' (the form of mercy I believe I was talking about), you will definitely not lose your reward.

Another reason why Socialism is hated (if you read all the previous bracketed wordings), is because the Devil knows the similarities of Socialism with regards to the goals of God (that may help the world see a correctness to it and by means of understanding Socialism, connect it to the existence of a Godly realm) and tries to intoxicate the understanding of Socialism by creating the ideology of Communism and Marxism which enforces an evil connotation brought towards the fundamental Socialist mindset. Also using Democracy to be a part of human ideology and indirectly **making the world feel** like freedom is the way out towards a better living standard, all the while, unbeknownst to the world that by entering Democracy, the world ends up becoming vulnerable to the acts of evil by their fellow human beings with various self-interests, and this brings about the understanding that life is difficult to live and because people understand that life is difficult to live, when they somehow manage to obtain life on earth, they end up with values that in turn damages society rather than having a willingness to share the life that they had obtained. The opposing angels that are against God, want these various mindsets to exist within the human understanding that is why the Bible says that: "We (the human being) wrestle not against flesh and blood but against powers and principalities in high places." The Bible says this because it isn't a physical battle but rather it is a battle of values. God who is good wants us to have good values and remain in God by retaining those good values no matter what the world throws at us because behind the scenes there is an unseen explanation where the opposing angels are elaborately orchestrating a worldwide plan to prove a point to God. In other words, there are unseen forces that want to change our mindset and those forces will stop at nothing to prove that they are true and correct because they strongly believe in what they believe to be true. And at the consummation of all things or at the end of the world, God will punish those (the human beings) who although were made in the image and likeness of God (which supposedly mean that they should unconsciously have good values in the first place), yet succumb to the wits of the forces of evil into believing lies, half-truths and is found to side with bad values, and together with the opposing angels, bring them all to an eternal place of punishment. But to all those who stay true to having good values will enter into the Kingdom of God, where they shall live with their creator forever.

Coming back to the first paragraph again, if the existence of the Kingdom of God can be seen as something that is similar to how wise Socialists were capable of coming up with Socialism **through a human way of thinking** (through a logical human understanding of things to tackle the crisis of conflicting values that exists in the world), then we should be able to conclude that this is proof enough of the existence of an intellectual fact to sustain the reasoning of the existence of a good God and his goal for societal harmony and continual coexistence.

4. The Incomprehension For The Need Of A Sacrifice (Jesus Christ) In The Christian Religion.

THE DEATH OF Jesus Christ was God asking for mercy by conveying something to the people. God is saying, "As a last resort, because your evil deeds on the earth that causes me, the creator, who is goodness itself, to be angry because you are supposed to be my people, created in my image, and having my goodness found in you, but instead, you choose the side of evil; Therefore as a last resort, I who is God gave myself as a sacrifice to see if you would be content with my death."

In the courses of life, when a mother does not know what to do with her son, where her son wants something but the mother says no to him over and over again, but he still insists on marrying a girl his mother disapproves of, what will the mother do in desperate need, out of her love for her son, to have him not marry that girl? The mother will say, "I love you, my son, yet if you continue on with your wants and wishes that go beyond what I believe is good for you, then let me die right now, that in death I will no longer know you and hence be free of my conscience to want to stop you from going against my wishes." This is something that describes what God is doing with the sacrifice of Christ. God is saying, "Have mercy on me child, for I am your God and creator and

319

knows what is best for you for I am goodness itself." By self-sacrifice, God is hoping that with his death being witnessed by the child, the child will realize that he ended up losing his mother because he insists on marrying the girl. God wants the people to realize that God who is good and knows what is good for the people, chose death to give people life, in hopes that once people see the good God's death, they will realize that they have killed their God because of the evil they had chosen to do and then admit that they are wrong in choosing evil, which causes goodness to fade away (when you choose evil, logically speaking, you are asking for goodness to fade away), and having admitted and realizing what they had done, they will throw evil away and strive to do good and once they have done good, and realize the wisdom behind being good, they will achieve everlasting life.

And so Jesus Christ who is said to be God incarnate (which may mean has the same values & way of thinking as God), died on the cross, to give a statement to the world. And because of the death of Jesus Christ, now no longer do man talk with God directly (for in a sense God who is goodness itself has been made to fade away by the choice of evil done by man), but instead because Christ rose from the dead (as proclaimed to be seen by eyewitnesses which may not be scientific evidence but having multiple eyewitnesses in history does mean that something did happen but if no one will believe that, then what we can do is we make 'the existence of the multiple eyewitnesses' to be brought up as the eighth hypothesis in this understanding in the existence of God) and because of that would mean to have won the battle against Death and Hades (which we know that once we die, Hades usually holds us in and never lets us go), Jesus Christ is lifted up by God to the point where Christ is seen as God because God has said, "Now, no man shall come unto me unless, my Son (who have done what i wanted to be done and was the only one who could do it for me), has ordained that person to be worthy (in the eyes of my Son)." This makes the Son, Jesus Christ, to become the intercessor of God and man. And so Christians who believe, actually pray to Jesus Christ, in the hopes that their prayers will be handed over to God from the hands of Jesus Christ. And so it is written that Christ said, "Whoever so ask for anything, in my name, will the Father provide, for my name's sake." Because Christ indeed suffered and died to subdue the anger of God and so God gave Jesus Christ the authority to sit on his right side (giving him the authority over heaven and earth but still remain second to God just as how Joseph the beloved son of Israel was second to Pharaoh) and also all Jesus Christ required of you and me is to believe in Jesus Christ as a means to say that if you believe in the Son (who is also conforming to goodness or represents goodness itself for the Son has the value and mindset of goodness itself), you will strive to do good in your life; and because you who truly believe in Jesus Christ, will, sure enough, be good in your life, it will definitely show in your works and actions, then you upon death, will be judged based on your actions and those who are deemed to have done well will enter the future Kingdom of God. And so in the Christian world, God requires 1 thing and that is the belief of Jesus Christ and what he did on the cross. Blind faith does not save the man. But rather true faith which is the belief of Jesus Christ truly and honestly believe in Christ is the thing that will bring about the longing to live just as how Christ lived on the earth, in other words, to live a Godly life hence automatically you receive everlasting life. But because God required Jesus Christ as the being that provided the salvation, being good only is not enough to God (or in the eyes of God) but the world also needs to believe in Jesus Christ (as ordained by God, the mighty one and above all things and so have the authority of requiring this requirement from his creations). But if on the day of judgment Jesus Christ decided to have a say to God, to allow those who did not believe in him but have good works to also enter into the Kingdom of God, I believe Jesus Christ could ask for it (I mean God did give him the authority to ask God for anything, so he could ask for it and it may be given). That is why it is written that after the thousand years was over, and when Hades and Death would give up the dead in them and the people who have died from (the time of) the foundations of the world has been brought back to life, they will be judged according to their works, without continuing to imply the need to have believed in Jesus Christ. Therefore my understanding and theory of God, is that goodness (which God claims that He is goodness itself) is good because Jesus Christ (who also conforms to goodness itself) in the end having been given the authority of God, may allow people who have been good and have chosen goodness, even those outside of Christianity, to enter the Kingdom of God, whilst those who are literally wicked all their life will enter the lake of fire along with Death and Hades. And now we can come to the conclusion as an intellectual being, having been given the human understanding of God, confirms that (1) God exists, (2) God is good, and also (3) God created mankind, the world, and all things within.

5. The Inability To Understand The Trinity Found In Christian Doctrine.

THE LOGICAL WAY of understanding the doctrine of the trinity is to understand it to mean as having the same values and mindset. When they say 3 people are one, like I said previously in one of the parentheses found in this book, 'One' does not mean one and the same. 'One' means to have the same mind, the same way of thinking. It is found in Socialism, because Socialism is a collective of people building up society together in harmony, that Socialism requires a society that conforms to the same understanding of life — this is a people with the same values & way of thinking. Therefore, the word 'One' that is used by Jesus Christ (1) to define him and God, (2) to define him and his disciples, and (3) to define him and God and his disciples, as is found in the contents of his prayer before his death, can be replicated in our human understanding, as is understood by the human authors of Socialism, as to mean having the same mind, and values, and way of thinking. This understanding that I have written about the trinity will be able to help the reader to understand this whole chapter that I have written to Atheists and other readers who end up reading this, which could have been guided by some power of God.

6. Final Remarks Concerning The Previous 5 Points Presented In This Chapter

To THE ATHEISTS reading this, or to other readers, this is all I can say to bring about an understanding towards the Christian religion. I believe the hatred that Marx had towards religion is wrong because religion actually brings good values to society. And this whole chapter tries to bring a scientific explanation to the existence of God because a true Atheist (having a strong disbelief towards God) that wants to help the world (as was the intention of Karl Marx) will end up destroying the world instead.

I started this chapter with the goal of changing good atheist people to have a view to not end up hating religion but as can be seen from the 5 points discussed, I end up trying to help readers understand Christianity. I do not know to what extent the people of science and those with logical thinking, will be able to understand; but as a Socialist who yearns for Socialism, out of human understanding and wisdom to rid the world of evil and bring about the existence of a society in harmony which inevitably achieves continual co-existence, the proof of the existence of a God can be proven and I believe I have just logically proven it.

How exactly you may ask. It is by providing you with an intellectual understanding of the need for coexistence, that even the cosmos and the elements therein have been known to be doing all this time. (And I believe that the people of Science know that the elements do coexist by themselves that is why harmony is found in nature. The ants for example have a oneness that is why they coexist but we humans have instead a diversity of values because of a lack of understanding towards what is good, what is wise, and the lack of understanding needed to grasp the idea towards coexistence because of the will of choice that is given to us that causes us to make the wrong choices for ourselves and for our societies.) Therefore when a logical thinking human being comes along and tries his best to build a society (based on his understanding of the ugliness of human beings whereby each have their own will of choice to do what they want) that has a mindset towards coexistence, which yearns to bring about goodness and the oneness towards that good mindset that will bring us all together in harmony, **comma**, which matches the natural science found in the universe, which is coexistence, **again comma**, where on the other hand, God who is supposedly known as the creator of all things, proposes human beings to submit themselves to His laws of goodness created by His wisdom, (to bring about the same oneness that science itself sees and understand within their study of the elements) as to bring about a form of coexistence whereby when the human themselves have gotten the same enlightenment as God, then only does God allow humans to coexist with Him, **comma**, **therefore** when both Socialism and God have the same goal of bringing about the coexistence that science itself still cannot comprehend the reason why the elements in the universe have to depend on one another in order for the science to work, **therefore**, **because** the understanding of the galaxy and the science thereof needs that factor of coexistence which is replicated by our understanding of the type of society needed to bring about harmony which is talking about that same coexistence, **therefore** the reasoning behind the existence of God, who yearns also for the unification of society to be one with God so as to coexist just as how the elements that make up the galaxies themselves coexist, **a deduction can be made valid** to the existence of God.

(Let me pause and educate the reader as to why I cannot place a full stop when trying to connect the dots above. Because when I put a full stop when trying to connect the dots between Socialism, the galaxy itself that conforms to the rules of Socialism, and the God that is supposed to have created the galaxy itself does in fact bring about Socialism, and where all these 3 things connect together in a sense where a form of coexistence must exist in order to bring about an eternal, continual harmony, the moment I put a full stop between them, I will not be able to convey the information I want to present to you, as intended.)

Let me try to rephrase once again, (1) Socialism, which is the goal whereby the people in society conforms to the same mindset and values of goodness, as is needed to coexist without fail, **along with** (2) the study of Science, where a coexistence is found to be needed for the science itself to work, **and** (3) the ambitions of God, despite the opposition of the angels, have prepared laws based on the best form of wisdom there is, where whosoever obeys the law and follows in the footsteps of God by choosing to be good rather than to be bad, hence achieving coexistence with the creator Himself; it is because, the word 'coexistence' is the final goal for perfect harmony that brings about an agreement of working together to achieve the continual everlasting workings of things, which is found in all 3 cases, therefore when men of science and men of logical thinking can agree to (1) the workings of science itself, and (2) the workings of Socialism, both the men of science and men of logical thinking, should also be able to agree and accept, the existence of God because all of the 3 came down to the same conclusion **that** for the need of coexistence, we would first need a oneness in mind that brings about the working together done amongst the subjects of each of the three cases; where (1) the subjects of Socialism consists of members of society, (2) the subjects of God consists of His creations + Himself, and (3) the subjects of science consists of the elements, atoms, particles, etc. that they are studying.

(Because the existence of God follows the principle of what we know as nature, we should be able to accept that type of logic **that does not go against** our understanding of nature, **just because** it didn't go against it. All this time, people always debunk the existence of God. But now, with the co-relation to the two subjects having been presented : (1) what we know as science, and (2) what we know as God; if you allow yourself to believe in science, allow yourself to believe also in God.)

In fact, I believe that God who seeks coexistence with mankind, created the earth and everything therein with the same laws of coexistence. In other words, for God, being the being who needs the coexistence between Himself and His human creations, which is why He made the laws required for mankind to obey and learn the goodness to being good (represented by the 10 commandments where man is told to love God & also love one another), which is a pre-requisite for people living in coexistence with one another, then, if this same God indeed created the universe, he would have created it using the same principles of coexistence, in which we have seen and known the universe to be like.

But if what I say about science does not make sense or is untrue (because I am not a man of science), therefore we would now get down to talk **only about** Socialism and God. If my theories of Socialism can be understood, by the people of Science and people of logically thinking, as a means to achieve harmony and coexistence, I would end up needing society to conform to a oneness of goodness by restricting their freedom in order to achieve it, **comma**, therefore because I have proven that God also tends to achieve harmony and coexistence by hoping that the people cling to goodness despite whatever the world throws at them, **comma**, would you be willing to believe in the existence of that good God, who does all things and because He does not want anyone to perish or be condemned to hell, He does not instantly kill those who do wrong but let them live so as to be able to reflect and repent of their actions, He does all these things, so that we may come into a good understanding of seeking to do good so that we may one day be allowed to live with God who is goodness itself. Once again I ask, will you be willing to believe in that good God?

I would like to simply leave it at that.

VII. Final Words & Contact Information

INFORMATION CONCERNING THE AUTHOR, COMMENTARIES & HIS LAST WORDS

ALTHOUGH THE READER may not agree on all of the topics that I presented in this book, but I find this book quite mind-opening. I am certain that I have opened perspectives unto how the reader could view the world and understand what's going on in the world — the actions that are being done, what are the various things that impact how an action is done, and so on and so forth.

I could have written some misconceptions; the book could have some inaccuracies but I hope valuable information or knowledge has been obtained from this reading. Most of all, I hope the reader, having read this book, and with the opening of the mind, may strive to seek out wisdom to understand life itself and strive to make some good use of it that we may be fruitful and be a blessing to our respective societies.

As for myself, I would like to try to be able to bring about a Socialist society within my lifespan. Money is one of the factors preventing me from achieving it though. Like all the other early Socialist people, I am finding for like minded-people who strongly agree with how a Socialist environment may help the suffering people in the world to find a home and a city that cares for them. I would like to share my email here for the purpose of gathering like-minded people, where further discussions can be done and an action plan could be formulated. Please also include the subject title: Like-Minded Towards Socialistic City. My email is as follows: erick.kasih@gmail.com

Secondly, I am also finding for people who are willing to donate to build this city. Because it's not going to be a small sum. The city building would probably be faced with much difficulty in all the aspects of realizing my hope of bringing about the first Socialistic city and in every process along the way, but because I do not want this book to be just a book of knowledge and discussion but also a book that brings people together to envision a safe haven where people are obliged to be good to one another and where the system that will be created to self-govern the people itself supports the notion that society will be good to one another, therefore I am strongly in want of realizing this big hope for our future human civilization. To bluntly admit it, I need the funding and if you so happen of being rich enough in paper money and at the same time see what I am hoping to build as something good (as defined by your being and consciousness), then I would like to receive donations (in other words, non-binding investments) from you and you will automatically be included in the group of like-minded people. You can reach me using the same email above with the subject title: Funds For Socialistic City Building.

If you have critics, please use the subject title: Critics - Socialist Book. I will reply only if I feel the need to address your critic, if not then your critic, being a word of criticism (meant and invented to be a one-sided closed statement), doesn't actually need a reply.

As for inquiries, use the subject title: Inquiries - Socialist Book - [followed by the main point of the issue you wanted to ask]. As for the email body: state your inquiries in detail. Then send it to the email address provided above.

Lastly, If after reading this book, the readers come up with a name for myself (the writer and author of this book entitled 'Preferring Socialism Over Democracy : Envisioning Cities Of Societal Harmony & Continual Coexistence'), please do not call me the 'Father of Socialism'. But rather I prefer the title, 'The Socialist Prince (of South-East Asia)'.

[Additional serious writings that relates to the Preface : Coming back to the Preface where I stated that the world was made to appreciate Democracy yet hate Socialism or in other words made to appreciate freedom yet dislike restrictions, this is done to ready the world for something.

We should be able to believe, given my previous writings, that the one instigating this event is the devil because it is only through freedom that the devil will be able to fulfill his plans. It is because of the existence of those evil unseen forces, which consists of those angelic beings or heavenly beings who are in opposition to God, that those people who promote and strongly defend freedom and democracy actually are doing so in the favor of the evil one. And so people like myself are hated because what I am doing is actually opening the eyes of fellow human beings to understanding that good restrictions are what we ought to do in order to be in coexistence with one another which is what the creator of heaven and earth required of us to do & be against the evil one that opposes the mindset of goodness and wisdom. But those people who hate me are blinded by the freedom that the devil promotes the world to have because the devil is against the restrictions that God wants man to have over themselves to protect themselves from being evil people.

Maybe to most readers, what I am saying seems farfetched because I am saying that there is this big bad mastermind that is unbelievable for anyone in their right mind to believe in the first place. I know that first of all I have to make you believe that God exists and then I have to make you believe that there is an opposition in heaven towards God because of the self-interest of some of the heavenly beings towards God. And then I have to imply that freedom is what the opposition towards God wants whereas God who is good and wise is against the freedom that the devil wants heaven to have. And so it is kind of hard to believe what I am saying. But if we think of it the way I see it. Once again, if you have a very good leader that wants the coexistence of mankind, because mankind is filled with fleshly desires, impulses, selfish tendencies, filled with emotions, some of whom are naive and weak-minded, some of whom are easily swayed to perverted understandings, some of whom fills their minds with evil because they were done evil by others since birth, etc., therefore the leader will prefer to set laws in motion that restricts all these bad human actions that may appear from appearing in society and doing harm to others.

Let's assume that God does exist and that God is both goodness itself and wisdom itself. And mankind is filled with evil in their hearts and minds, and so what will such a God do to ensure that His creations live proper lives and treat their fellow citizens kindly and with much care. I believe he would give them laws to follow; laws that are different from secular laws; laws that enter into the personal life of the individual to prevent them from hurting their fellow people of God. That is what most religions have, laws that enter into the personal life of the individual to restrict them from doing things that are bad for them to do.

I have this notion of thought that in most cases, those who are wise will instruct people to do something or instruct people not to do something. But because they are too wise they forget to explain the reasoning for the existence of those instructions. They just say, "These are the laws, follow them to the letter and we will all live happily ever after." In most cases, it is true that when you follow the instructions of a truly wise person you will live happily ever after. But like I said before, everyone who is given a mind to think will inevitably be curious as to those instructions. First of all, an instigator will appear and stir up others to be as curious as he is, and once he has amassed a large group of people, they will start opposing the need for those laws or instructions. It's similar to what I am doing here. I am telling people, "Look, Democracy is not what you think it is; it is actually allowing you to agree to hate restrictions even though the leader giving those restrictions is a very good and loving person." And also likewise the devil I believe said to the other angels, "Hey, we are not going to live like this forever right? If God is going to rule forever, He is being authoritative. Well, shouldn't there be some kind of fairness amongst us, if God indeed wants us to live with Him." In the case of the devil, he opposes the laws of heaven that teach goodness and wisdom and incites others to have his view. In my case, I oppose Democracy because we human beings are prone to doing acts of evil and are not yet ready for Democracy; as a logical thinking person, I believe we should first learn and understand what is good and what is bad yet choose to do good and then you can choose whichever ideology you want to live under. But the problem is, as long as we continue to have children, as long as evil lingers within us, to ensure that people do not harm their fellow people, we should not go near Democracy; in other words, restricting ourselves is the wisest thing to do.]

Words Directed To The World & All Its Inhabitants Therein

Preferring Socialism Over Democracy : Envisioning Cities Of Societal Harmony & Continual Coexistence

---

To THE WORLD, I say, "The Only True Religion, Is The One That Tries To Bring About Coexistence (By Means Of Wisdom Found Within Its Understanding (Of Which Goodness Is Strived To Be Achieved))."

"Socialism, although it seeks for coexistence, is not a religion, but a mindset made by man. Religion is something that has a supernatural God in it that has existed from the dawn of time. Now, from all the religions there are in existence, find one and make your choice. Pick your side!"

"If self-interest exists within us, likewise can it exist within all things that are living that have a conscience of choice. And therefore we can believe in the existence of a powerful group of spiritual beings, that are also given the conscience of choice, and have chosen opposition to wisdom and goodness, and has been trying to bring about falsehood into the world so that we human beings will fail to see the goodness and the existence of a living God. (They do all the means possible to trick us into believing lies, and truths that have any percentage of lies in them, to make us doubt. They guide us, who are logical in nature, to understand a logic that they themselves have invented to disprove the existence of the ONE they are in opposition to.)"

LASTLY, I BESEECH YOU to purchase understanding from me that is given to those who seek understanding, "Idolatry, is the worship of God by means of bowing down to an object of creation. The right religion is the one whereby we bow and worship and give praise to the creator (without the means of an earthly object)."

"Pick a religion, but don't pick one blindly. Choose a religion that brings about the understanding needed for you to choose it in the first place. Choose a religion that tells you why you have to choose it and has made itself clear to you. Lastly, reason with yourself if whether or not it seeks for goodness and coexistence. If it does, then under the understanding that we have as human beings, who are a species that yearns and seeks for harmony along with coexistence with one another, that's the one we want for ourselves to have."

Closing Quote

Preferring Socialism Over Democracy : Envisioning Cities Of Societal Harmony & Continual Coexistence

---

"Now that you have read the book, read it once more that you may gain a better grasp on the understandings and truths found therein; especially the ultimate truth that leads you to the knowledge of an existing and good God."

Many Thanks To :

Caroline Michelon — Reedsy Illustrator, residing in Germany. She helped draw the front and back cover of the physical book and also the ebook.

The founders and employees of the following companies for assisting in the distribution of the contents of this book, throughout the world : Ingram Spark & Lightning Source, Amazon & KDP.

LPKN — for organizing a book writing workshop.

Giving An Online Book Review

Do you remember where you purchased this book from? If you purchased it from an online site, leaving a book review at their site may indirectly help strangers receive the same understanding you have received.

If you have found this book to be interesting or helpful, kindly do so. It also helps the book to stay afloat and easily spotted by book readers because of both your recommendation to read it & your ratings.

Thanks.

About the Author

A MIND WHO finds himself having Socialist tendencies & solutions when he started treading on the subject of World Economy & how money works, back in 2008. His journey was long and winding, but with much tenacity & a heart for humanity, he found the madness in society & deduced a solution for both social harmony within society & financial security for individuals.

THIS BOOK IS his first published book with the goal for a call to action towards like-minded people into realizing a city of safe haven made for good people who wants a better life for themselves, away from the wicked side of society, & are willing to do everything for the sake of their fellow neighbors in society.

THE AUTHOR IS given the name Jan Frederick Setyakasih. A wonderful name which means, the one loved by God, a peaceful ruler, and loyal in loving others. Surprisingly there are 22 letters in his name with a total accumulated value of 222 when using the normal alphabetical counter (eg. a=1; z=26).

A WONDERFUL NAME for a man with a wonderful hope and dream to create a better world for people who have been hit hard by wicked people and their wicked goals and self-interests. A man who yearns for peace and joy to be in abundance within society.

A FEW WORDS by the author, "I hope that understanding has flown from me to you. A mistaken word found here or there, does not make the whole book wrong. A wise man is open to rebuke and instruction. The wise is quick to listen and search for understanding but he also filters which is fit to be taken in and which is not fit. Likewise, I tell you, firstly, be humble enough to read with an open mind, then secondly, take in whatever you feel is right. Do the same for every piece of information that you read. Do not be quick to judge, do not fill yourself with arrogance, lest you end up missing out on crucial understandings. Lastly, I say, gain insight & understanding that truth may fill your mind; and then by means of having attained truth, love & forgive those who have done wrong towards you. The 3 types of evil people: (1) they who know not understanding, (2) they who do evil because they have been treated with evil, & (3) they who have chosen evil and do not want correction."

DO SHARE THE information begotten here with others that they too may inherit understanding.

JAN FREDERICK SK

(for those who want to follow my personal instagram, but be warned, i am a man of very few posts; i also use the same id for twitter and i try to be more active there : @jfskasih)